ISBN 978-1-330-73354-7
PIBN 10098409

For support please visit www.forgottenbooks.com

1 MONTH OF
FREE
READING

at

www.ForgottenBooks.com

By purchasing this book you are eligible for one month membership to ForgottenBooks.com, giving you unlimited access to our entire collection of over 1,000,000 titles via our web site and mobile apps.

To claim your free month visit:
www.forgottenbooks.com/free98409

English
Français
Deutsche
Italiano
Español
Português

www.forgottenbooks.com

Mythology Photography **Fiction**
Fishing Christianity **Art** Cooking
Essays Buddhism Freemasonry
Medicine **Biology** Music **Ancient**
Egypt Evolution Carpentry Physics
Dance Geology **Mathematics** Fitness
Shakespeare **Folklore** Yoga Marketing
Confidence Immortality Biographies
Poetry **Psychology** Witchcraft
Electronics Chemistry History **Law**
Accounting **Philosophy** Anthropology
Alchemy Drama Quantum Mechanics
Atheism Sexual Health **Ancient History**
Entrepreneurship Languages Sport
Paleontology Needlework Islam
Metaphysics Investment Archaeology
Parenting Statistics Criminology
Motivational

he

y Record.

Edited by E. T. BROWN.

Published First of Every Month.

80   Pages   80

Profusely Illustrated Throughout.   **Printed on Art Pap**

THE

Paper for Utility Poultry=Keepers.

PECIAL Correspondents in the UNITED KINGDOM,
COLONIES, EUROPE, and AMERICA.

☛ ON SALE AT ALL BOOKSTALLS OR NEWSAGENTS. ☚
Annual Subscription, **8/-** per Annum, post free.

end Post-Card to—
THE EDITOR, "Illustrated Poultry Record,"
15, Essex Street, Strand, W.C.,

FOR A FREE SPECIMEN COPY.

REPORT ON THE POULTRY INDUSTRY
IN BELGIUM.

National Poultry Organization Society.

REPORT ON

The Poultry Industry in Belgium.

BY

EDWARD BROWN, F.L.S.

Honorary Secretary of the National Poultry Organization Society;
Poultry Expert to the Agricultural Organization Society.

Author of " Report on the Poultry Industry in America,"
" Report on the Poultry Industry in Denmark and Sweden,"
" Poultry Keeping as an Industry for Farmers and Cottagers,"
" Races of Domestic Poultry," " Poultry Fattening, &c."

London :

NATIONAL POULTRY ORGANIZATION SOCIETY, LIMITED,

REGENT HOUSE, REGENT STREET, W.

1910.

National Poultry Organization Socie

LIMITED,

REGENT HOUSE, REGENT STREET, LONDON, W.

OBJECTS. The objects for the promotion of which the Society is established are: (*a*) The ization and development of the Poultry Industry as a most important branch of Agriculture; (*b*) the improvement of the quality and the increase quantity of eggs, poultry, &c., produced in the United Kingdom; maintenance of regularity and uniformity of supply; (*d*) the provision of facilities fo transit; and (*e*) the bringing of the producers and retailers into closer touch, in ord the best available market may be obtained at a minimum cost.

SCHEME OF OPERATIONS. The National Poultry Organization Society, Limited, endeavours to make more known the opportunities presenting themselves to farmers; affords practical informa to the class of poultry-keeping most suited to each district, having re the soil and the markets available; indicates the breeds which g best results; renders assistance in obtaining on the best terms app of a right kind; disseminates leaflets providing reliable information bearing upon the aspects of poultry culture; registers and supplies names of traders willing to t produce; keeps a register of poultry men and women desiring situations; and, ge assists the Branches and Depots, and through them individual breeders, in every possible.

BRANCHES AND COLLECTING DEPOTS. Branches of the Society are formed wherever the requisite local co-operation obtained. Many such branches have already been established, and are doing satis work in their respective districts, of which a list will be for on application to the Secretary. Where Collecting Dep formed, eggs are collected frequently, carefully tested, and are strictly fresh, branded with the Society's Trade Mark, packed and forwarded to ꜱ traders as rapidly as possible. By these means the quality is guaranteed, and produce placed in the front rank, yielding adequate returns to poultry-keepers. In ꜱ districts it is intended to encourage the improvement of Table Poultry, the quality of in many parts of the country is very deficient. By so doing it is hoped that en returns will be secured by breeders and raisers of poultry.

MEMBERSHIP. All subscribers to the National Poultry Organization Society, Limited, either d through any of its Branches, are Members of the Society, and entitled to its privilege scribers of One Guinea and upwards are registered as Members of in accordance with the Rules, which can be obtained on appl Subscriptions of One Shilling and upwards may be made to the Society or its Br Subscribers of not less than Five Shillings per annum and upwards receive the Journ

Copies of Leaflets for distribution, Forms of Application for Membership, and info respecting the work of the Society can be had from

The Secretary, National Poultry Organization Society, Limit
Regent House, Regent Street, Londo

TABLE OF CONTENTS.

		Page	Para.
INTRODUCTION		1	—
Objects of Enquiry		1	
Range of Tour...		2	
Results		3	
Acknowledgments		4	
I. POULTRY BREEDING IN BELGIUM ...		5	
General Conditions		5	
Modern Developments		6	2
Stock Breeding		6	3
Fancy Poultry		7	4
Historical		8	5
Poultry Farms...		9	6
Farm Poultry-keeping		10	7
Area and Population		11	8
Statistical		13	9
Improved Fertility of Land		14	10
A Changed District		15	11
Prosperity follows Poultry		15	12
Imports and Exports		16	13
II. HOUSING AND GENERAL MANAGEMENT		18	—
Simple Methods		18	14
Housing		19	15
Forms of Poultry Houses		19	16
The Colony House System		21	17
Hatching		21	18
Rearing...		22	19
Feeding...		23	20
Supplied Foods		24	21
Milk Sheep and Poultry		25	22
III. EGG PRODUCTION		26	—
A General Industry		26	23
Farm Work		27	24
The Braekel Country...		27	25
Sottegem		28	26
Braekels on Water Meadows		29	27
Renaix		30	28
Typical Examples		31	29

EGG PRODUCTION—*continued.*

		Page	Para.
A Breeding Farm		32	30
Poultry Allotments		32	31
Axioms on Poultry-keeping		33	32
The Campine		34	33
The Herve Country		35	34
Egg Farming		35	35
Italian Fowls as Layers		36	36
Size and Colour of Eggs		37	37
Average Production		38	38
Price of Eggs		39	39
Winter Supplies		39	40
IV. MARKET POULTRY		41	—
An Old Pursuit		41	41
Poulets de Lait		41	42
Poulets des Grains		42	43
Poulets de Bruxelles		43	44
The Table-poultry Area		44	45
Londerzeel		44	46
Methods Adopted		45	47
Hatching and Rearing		46	48
A Note of Warning		47	49
Fattening Establishments		47	50
No Cramming		48	51
Feeding and Killing		49	52
Poultry Farm at Lippeloo		50	53
Hatching at Lippeloo		51	54
Brooder Houses		51	55
Runs for Growing Birds		53	56
Results at Lippeloo		54	57
V. THE DUCK INDUSTRY		55	—
Duck Breeding		55	58
Huttegem and District		55	59
Ducklings and Chickens		56	60
Hatching and Rearing		57	61
A Spartan System		58	62
Water Lentils and Worms		59	63
Feeding the Ducklings		60	64
Laplaigne		60	65
Methods at Laplaigne		61	66
Feeding and Fattening		62	67
Lebbeke and Merchtem		62	68
VI. GEESE AND TURKEYS		64	—
Decline of the Goose		64	69
Few Turkeys		64	70
Ronquières		65	71
Turkey Breeding		66	72

GEESE AND TURKEYS—*continued.*

	Page	Para.
Methods of Management	67	73
Disposal of Ronquières Turkeys	68	74
A Turkey Fair...	69	75
Turkeys and Matrimony	69	76

VII. MARKETING THE PRODUCE ... ... 71 —

Nearness of Markets	71	77
No Co-operation	72	78
Egg Markets	73	79
Packing the Eggs	74	80
Preservation of Eggs...	74	81
Notes on Eggs...	75	82
Poultry Market at Audenarde	76	83
Malines Market	77	84
Brussels Market	77	85
Poultry Auctions	79	86

VIII. BELGIAN RACES OF POULTRY ... ... 80 —

Effects of Varied Conditions	80	87
Introduction of New Breeds	81	88
Distribution of Breeds	82	89
Qualities of Races	83	90
Braekel and Campine Fowls	84	91
Malines Fowl	84	92
Brabant Fowl	85	93
Ardenne Fowl	85	94
Herve Fowl	86	95
Rumpless Fowls	86	96
Utility Bantams	87	97
Cock-crowing Contests	88	98
Breeds of Ducks	89	99
Ronquières Turkey	90	100
Breeding Theories	91	101

IX. INSTRUCTION IN POULTRY-KEEPING ... 92 —

Lectures	92	102
Agricultural Colleges	93	103
Special Poultry Schools	94	104
Experimental Work	95	105

X. GENERAL NOTES ... ... 97 —

Intercommunications	97	106
Railway Rates...	98	107
National Federation of Poultry Societies ...	99	108
L'Union Avicole de Liége	100	109
Other Societies	100	110

XI. SUMMARY ... ... 102 —

Comparisons	102	111
Conclusions	103	112

ILLUSTRATIONS.

PLATE   I. IMPROVED CAMPINE FARM HOUSES ... *facing page* 16

   „   II. STRAW POULTRY HOUSE AT GRASHEIDE „   „   17

   „   III. BROODER HOUSE AT THIMISTER   ... „   „   24

   „   IV. MILK SHEEP IN POULTRY RUNS   ... „   „   25

   „   V. EXTERIOR OF FATTENING SHEDS AT LON-
         DERZEEL ...   . „   „   40

   „   VI. FATTENING CAGES ...   . „   „   41

   „   VII. A CARPENTER'S FLOCK OF MALINES ... „   „   48

   „   VIII. FIRST BROODER HOUSE AT LIPPELOO... „   „   49

   „   IX. DRUM BROODER AT LIPPELOO ...   ... „   „   52

   „   X. SECOND BROODER HOUSE AT LIPPELOO „   „   53

   „   XI. GROWING PENS AT LIPPELOO   ...   ... „   „   56

   „   XII. STRAW COOP FOR DUCKLINGS ...   ... „   „   57

   „   XIII. FLOCK OF HUTTEGEM DUCKLINGS WITH
         HEN   ...   . „   „   60

   „   XIV. ENCLOSURE FOR YOUNG DUCKS AT
         LAPLAIGNE   ...   . „   „   61

   „   XV. RONQUIÈRES TURKEYS   ...   . „   „   72

   „   XVI. MARKET SCENE AT AUDENARDE   ... „   „   73

REPORT

ON THE

Poultry Industry in Belgium.

To the Central Executive Committee of the
National Poultry Organization Society.

Ladies and Gentlemen,—

In continuance of the series of enquiries commenced in
1906, when I visited America, and in 1907, when present
conditions in Denmark and Sweden were investigated, in
respect to the poultry industry of the countries named,
I have made similar observations in Belgium during the
months of October, November, and December last. Here-
with I beg respectfully to submit my report, which, it may be
hoped, will prove of equal interest and value to those previously issued, and which have commanded a large measure
of attention in all parts of the civilized world.

OBJECTS OF ENQUIRY.—Probably there is no section of
Europe, and therefore of the world, where intensification of
method is carried out to the same degree as in Belgium,
which, with its dense population, its high standard of productiveness, and the general prosperity of its rural districts,
affords a wide field for investigation. It is equally true that
poultry-keeping enters more largely into Belgian farming
operations than in any other part of Europe, save a few
sections of France, where similar conditions prevail. I have
endeavoured to carry out your instructions, which were to
enquire into (1) the Belgian methods of production both of
eggs and table poultry; (2) the development of special breeds
of poultry whether as layers or for meat properties; (3) the
system of producing the famous *poulets de Bruxelles* and

poulets de lait (milk chickens) both as regards breeding and fattening ; (4) the duck industry of the Pays d'Alost ; (5) the effect which poultry-keeping has had on the fertility of the soil and general cultivation ; (6) the methods of marketing adopted, and (7) the steps taken by central and local authorities for encouragement of the industry, improvement of races of poultry, and by educational and experimental work.

RANGE OF TOURS.—With Belgium I have been fairly familiar for many years, but as considerable changes and developments have taken place in the last two decades, it was necessary that the ground should be covered completely. I have therefore taken two special journeys, in the course of which the greater part of the country was visited, including the Provinces of Flanders, east and west, Brabant, Hainaut, Namur, Antwerp, and Liége.   Visits were paid to the great egg-producing areas in Flanders, Antwerp, and Liége ; to the table-poultry districts between the city of Malines and Ghent on the one side, away to the Dutch border on the other ; to Audenarde and Laplaigne, where duck-raising is carried out so extensively, and to the Ronquières tableland, where turkeys bearing that name are bred.   Various markets were attended and many visits paid to farms, fattening and breeding establishments, &c.

RESULTS.—That the conditions met with in Belgium are, in many directions, peculiar to itself will be apparent by the report now submitted.   Great though the industrial and commercial developments in Belgium have been within recent years, creating an enormously increased demand for produce, that is by no means singular, for we find it the case to an even greater extent in Britain, America, and Germany. But it is essentially, outside a few areas, an agricultural country, with a peasantry deeply attached to the soil, possess-ing a knowledge of cultivation and breeding probably un-equalled by that of any other people.   Nearly every yard of ground which can be utilized productively is cultivated, and the relation of animal to plant life is realized to a degree which is highly commendable.   It is a striking fact that in spite of the growth of cities, towns, and manufacturing districts, this little country not only feeds itself, but has a considerable surplus for export to neighbouring countries, which is true as to eggs and poultry equally with other articles of food. The adaptability of the different races of poultry found within the borders of Belgium is remarkable, and its people have, in their own way, solved many problems which have not yet been reached in other lands. On the productive side there is much to learn from them, though, as I attempt to show in the report, there are methods which might not be so successful elsewhere, and which, in some cases, have been improved upon. In the summary given at the end of the report an attempt is made to indicate those systems worthy of emulation, more especially upon small holdings and allotments. One fact was impressed upon me on several occasions—namely, that at the basis of all efforts put forth is the ideal that " the prosperity of a country depends upon the position of its working people, not the rich alone; and, therefore, advancement of the former means enhanced demand for produce."

ACKNOWLEDGMENTS. — Adequate recognition of the great kindnesses and many courtesies extended to me is impossible, though in the report itself mention of some of these is made. Considerable interest was shown in my enquiry by officials, members of various societies, and private individuals, and my way was made easier thereby. His Excellency Mons. F. Schollaert, Belgian Minister of Agriculture, and the members of his staff supplied me with the statistics given and other information, to whom my heartiest thanks are due. My friend Mons. Louis Vander Snickt, Editor of *Chasse et Peche*, not only placed his encyclopædic knowledge at my disposal, making clear what might otherwise have been uncertain, and obtaining information which the somewhat secretive Flemish peasant would have refused to give to a stranger—for they are by no means communicative on such questions—and securing me most valuable introductions, but he generously accompanied me to the various centres, at a great expenditure of his time and energy. He is so well known that his presence opened every door. Madame Van Schelle has helped me greatly in respect to the Province of Antwerp. To M. Maurice

Laloux, of Liége, I was indebted for taking me in his motor over part of the Ardennes country, enabling me to visit places otherwise unattainable except at considerable expenditure of time.   For permission to reproduce the photographs which form Plates XIII., XIV., and XV., I am indebted to Mons. Vander Snickt.

I have the honour to remain,
Ladies and gentlemen,
Your obedient servant,
EDWARD BROWN.

Regent House, Regent Street, W.,
January, 1910.

REPORT

ON THE

Poultry Industry in Belgium.

I.—POULTRY-BREEDING IN BELGIUM.

1. GENERAL CONDITIONS.—Small though the modern
kingdom of Belgium is in extent, it presents remarkably
diversified conditions, both as to the conformation of the land,
the methods of cultivation adopted, and the inhabitants. It
includes the flat plains of Flanders, Antwerp, and Hainaut,
varying greatly in the quality of the soil, though the larger
part is rich and highly productive, the undulating districts of
Brabant and Limbourg, where, in some cases, the elevation
is considerable, and the mountainous sections of the Provinces of Liège, Belgian Luxembourg, and Namur, including
what is known as the Ardennes. With the exception of the
higher lands in Brabant, Liége, Namur and Luxembourg,
the farms are small, or moderate, in extent, and intensification of production is met with to a degree found in few other
parts of Europe. As is usually the case, on the smaller
occupations poultry-keeping is most developed, though within
recent years there has been a vast increase in the number of
fowls maintained upon larger farms, whereon this branch
of live stock has proved highly profitable. Equally varied
is the people themselves, for we find Flemish ranging from
the Dutch border across the Pays d'Alost to France, extending into that country. Lille is the centre of what is known
as French Flanders, where, in the rural districts, Flemish
is still the language of the people. South and east of
Brussels wc come upon the great area inhabited by the
Walloons, French speaking, and showing in their physique
and mental development the influence of their environment.

In speaking of Belgium, therefore, we must remember that, though the area is small, it embraces highly diversified conditions, natural, physical, and economic.

2. MODERN DEVELOPMENTS.—For centuries the Netherlands has occupied an important position in Western Europe, and its people early attained that prosperity which follows great industry. Study of the history of the country shows that vast wealth was accumulated hundreds of years ago, and that the Trade Guilds exerted an important influence before the time of the Spanish dominion. The remarkable industrial developments of recent years, as seen in the manufacturing centres and the growth of the port of Antwerp, have created a demand for produce which, but for the industry of the rural population and their realization of the opportunity presented to them, could not have been met by home supplies. In many directions, not only does Belgium provide for her own needs, but also has a margin for export. As shown below, that is the case in connection with poultry and eggs, the production of which has increased enormously within recent years, and is now an important factor in the agriculture of the country. One fact has impressed me very much—namely, that whilst in some directions the methods adopted appear antiquated and show no signs of progression, in others great advances have been made, some of which are especially suggestive where smaller farms and occupations are met with. Under those conditions intensification must take place to yield an adequate return, and I know of no country which offers a finer example of great production in accordance with the amount of land available. Whilst it is unquestionable that the standard of life is lower in many parts of Belgium than we are accustomed to see in Britain, it is higher than in some sections of Scotland and Ireland. That standard, however, is determined by habit rather than want of means, for the evidence is that the Belgian peasantry own more money than their manner of life would indicate.

3. STOCK-BREEDING.—Some time ago I wrote that[1] ' There is no part of Europe where the peasantry have

---

[1] " Races of Domestic Poultry," 1906, p. 112.

shown greater skill in the production of valuable races of animals and birds, or have given more intelligent attention to the improvement upon practical lines, than in the Low Countries, more especially—as a result of favourable conditions—in what is now known as Belgium. The inhabitants of that land are essentially practical. Their industry and thrift are proverbial." Present observations have abundantly confirmed that statement. For many centuries the Belgians have given themselves to the work of breeding. Restricted by limitations of space, their attention has not been devoted so much to larger races of stock, as in Britain and elsewhere, as to the smaller animals and birds. The result is seen in the number of breeds of poultry met with, each specially suited to the soil and conditions found within a given area, in which the characteristics have been individualized and the qualities highly developed. Information as to these is given in a later chapter. So far as my knowledge goes there is no country, save perhaps the adjoining Kingdom of Holland, where an equal number of native breeds are to be found on the same extent of territory. The breeding instincts of the Belgian people find expression in other directions. There the Homing pigeon has been developed for its powers of flight. These birds are to be seen everywhere, and the sport is national. I was told that in connection with pigeon races more money is won on a single day than is awarded as prizes for horses in a whole year. Further, the breeding of canaries and cage birds is also very popular. Undoubtedly, the settlement of Netherlanders around Norwich during the time of Spanish religious persecution explains why that city is the greatest centre for canary breeding in England. Another instance is the breeding of rabbits, which animals are kept to an enormous extent, the skins from which form an important part of the industry and trade of Alost. One dealer at Lebbeke informed me that he had sold nearly 100,000 such skins within a short period. What is the case with animals and birds is equally true in respect to plant life.

4. FANCY POULTRY.—Whilst it is true that the Belgians are practical in the extreme, there is a large amount of what may be termed fancy breeding in that country. Nor is this

a modern development. It would appear that for centuries throughout the Netherlands breeding for external characteristics, or abnormal types, or for sport, has been general. To that we owe several varieties of poultry, pigeons and cage birds, some of which, notably the Cropper pigeon and the Belgian canary, are altogether abnormal. The same tendency is strongly in evidence at the present time, for, as shown later, there are breeders devoting themselves entirely to production of extreme types. In no other country on the Continent of Europe has the English exhibition system been so widely copied as in Belgium, where great shows are held at Brussels, Antwerp, Ghent, Liége, and elsewhere. The results are that practical and fancy poultry breeders are sharply divided. The former are the food producers, the latter chiefly those who breed for pleasure or business. The fanciers have introduced many new breeds, but with one or two exceptions they have had comparatively little influence upon the farmers and peasants, the latter of whom especially will never show a bird or buy exhibition stock. Fanciers are chiefly well-to-do people, or the working-class communities in the industrial districts. One section of poultry-keepers, those who compete in the cock-crowing contests, are chiefly artizans, but that is a sport, as is cock-fighting. Large numbers of game fowls are bred for the last-named purpose. Although prohibited in Belgium, I fear a good deal of cocking goes on, and, as it is permitted in Northern France, devotees have only to travel a few miles to indulge in their pastime without fear of gendarmes and the law. We see, therefore, that the Belgians are a race of poultry-breeders for one purpose or another.

5. HISTORICAL.—It is evident that the breeding of poultry has been carried out for many centuries. The claim has been that for more than a thousand years have poultry been bred and produced on what may be termed industrial lines; that is, systematically and for food production. When it is remembered that the people of Brussels in 1054 were called " Kickefritters " (chicken-eaters), there is fair evidence in support of this statement. But we can go further back, to the time of Charlemagne (eighth century), for at that period all millers on the banks of streams were com-

pelled to keep ducks, and farmers to keep poultry, as they had to pay tribute in fowls, ducks, and carp to the land, or overlord. Through dynastic and other influences the Low Countries were for many centuries brought into direct communication with Burgundy, Germany, Austria, Italy, and Spain, and her great prosperity for a considerable period of time would encourage a pursuit such as poultry-keeping. It would appear that here, as in many other countries, the rise of abbeys and monasteries led to the dissemination of new and better breeds, first introduced to meet the needs of the monks themselves, and afterwards were distributed over the surrounding district. What were the classes of poultry then kept we have no means of knowing. So far as evidence is available it can be accepted that, in spite of the prolonged conflict which led to throwing off the Spanish yoke, there was a great increase of poultry-breeding in Belgium within the sixteenth and seventeenth centuries, of which the present is but a natural development and evolution. It will be seen, therefore, that the conditions are entirely different from those recorded in my Reports on America in 1906 and Denmark in 1907, in both of which countries, as to a lesser extent in our own, poultry-keeping as an industry has had to be built up from the basis, for in Belgium it has existed for a long period of time as a definite branch of farming. That fact should be kept in view as the following pages are read, for it will explain much that would otherwise be misunderstood.

6. POULTRY FARMS.—Poultry-farming, that is, the keeping of large numbers of fowls on a limited area either for egg or meat production, is practically unknown in Belgium, though various attempts have been and are being made in that direction. Near the Dutch border is a Trappist Monastery where 4,000 laying hens are kept, and at another of these communities in the Province of Antwerp is a smaller plant, at which the stock consists entirely of White Leghorns. The statement is made that at the latter a profit of 6,000 francs (£240) per annum has been realized. These are both stated to produce only for market and do not depend upon the sale of stock birds or eggs for hatching. The enterprise of the Vicomte de Beughem at Lippeloo is a very interesting

development. It is entirely for the production of chickens for the fatteners, but, as it is upon special lines and the breeding stock are in the hands of farmers and others, it differs greatly from an ordinary poultry farm. Further particulars of this plant are given in another chapter. Some time ago at Haeltert, in Flanders, the rearing of chickens on a large scale was attempted by means of shelf brooders, as described by Madame Van Schelle in a paper read before the Second National Poultry Conference in 1907, but it was not a financial success, and has since been abandoned. I heard of a few other places where something is being tried in this way, but as a rule they may be termed breeding establishments rather than poultry farms, and, in accordance with our own experience in the United Kingdom, America, and elsewhere, to meet the increased expenditure of such places they must secure a greater return than is possible for purely market produce. That they are valuable in relation to the industry as a whole, as breeding centres, cannot be questioned. If poultry-farming *pur et. simple* can be made to pay anywhere, it should be in Belgium, where labour is cheap, food not higher than in our own country, and the demand for and prices of eggs and poultry regular and high. It is very suggestive, therefore, that up to the present no important developments on these lines have taken place. It may be thought that some of the instances recorded in this report, more especially where the operations are small, such as the Renaix district, can fairly be included in the term poultry-farming, but these are supplemental to other work and not a means of livelihood. Many similar cases can be recorded in our own country.

7. FARM POULTRY-KEEPING.—Speaking generally, with the exception of the hilly districts of the Provinces of Liége, Namur, and Luxembourg, in the last two of which the population is scanty, Belgium is a huge poultry farm. In what is known as the Ardennes the country is thinly populated, and largely devoted to sport. There fowls are kept chiefly for household purposes, but are increasing in number. Fowls and ducks are to be met with everywhere in the other provinces ; not, it is true, massed in great numbers upon one place, but scattered over the land, each farm maintaining

a good stock. In no country with which I am acquainted, save certain parts of England and the Little Compton district of Rhode Island in America, are so many fowls to be seen from the road or railway as in Belgium. Not only is that so in Flanders and Antwerp, but on the larger farms to the east and south of Brussels, in Brabant, I was very much impressed by the great increase in poultry-keeping as compared with a few years ago. An interesting feature in connection with these farms is referred to later. I was informed at Sottegem, which is the centre of a great egg-producing district, that several farmers are largely increasing their stock of poultry, finding them more profitable than anything else, in some cases keeping as many as 300 to 400 layers. Some of the smaller occupiers are giving up their fields to poultry and the growing of crops for them, which may succeed up to a given, though, unfortunately, by no means a certain, point, but has elements of risk in it. The old Flemish saying that " three hens will help to keep you, but you must keep six hens," by which was meant that where three could find their own living six would need feeding, has been disproved or forgotten. That, however, was in the days when prices were probably a fourth of what are now obtainable. I suppose the Belgians will have to learn the same lesson as others—namely, that the balance between animal and plant life must be maintained, and that increase of the former at expense of the latter must bring about disease and loss. With the exception, however, of a few examples in the Londerzeel district, where, it seemed to me, concentration is being carried to the danger point, it can be conceded that up to the present they have successfully accomplished the intensification of method and of numbers, and have abundantly proved that poultry-keeping on smaller occupations can take an important share in the total result. It is estimated that at the present time not less than 10 per cent. of the land in the Pays d'Alost is occupied by poultry, the rest being given up to cultivation. As a rule, the farms in that section are from 10 to 15 acres in extent. There is, however, a very large number of smaller occupiers.

8. AREA AND POPULATION.—The total area of Belgium is 11,373 square miles, which is about equal to the counties of Hertford, Lancashire, Lincolnshire, and Yorkshire, and the

population on December 31, 1905, was 7,238,622. It is one
of the most densely populated countries in the world, with
636 inhabitants to the square mile. The following figures,
for which I am indebted to the courtesy of the Belgian
Minister of Agriculture, give the statistics as to the respective
provinces :—

Province	Area in hectares	Population, December 31, 1905	Number of inhabitants per square mile
Antwerp	283,175	926,624	850
Brabant	328,289	1,415,090	1,120
West Flanders ...	323,383	859,576	691
East Flanders ...	300,400	1,095,006	949
Hainaut	372,166	1,211,947	847
Liége	289,473	878,346	787
Limbourg	241,187	261,702	283
Luxembourg ...	441,784	229,143	135
Namur	366,024	381,118	257
Totals	2,945,503	7,238,622	636

The population per square mile in the United Kingdom
was 367, so that Belgium has a density of 72½ per cent. greater.
The above table includes the cities, and to that extent does
not represent the rural districts. For instance, Antwerp
Province comprises the great port of that name, Brabant
embraces Brussels with its 600,000 inhabitants, and Liége
not only the city but the collieries and iron districts adjacent.
But Flanders contains no great cities, and the average there
largely represents a rural population. As already indicated,
Belgium is a land of small occupations. The census to be
taken at the end of the current year will bring the information up to date, but the following figures, showing the
distribution of the land, is taken from the agricultural
statistics for 1895 :—

Area[1]	No. of Holdings	Percentage
Half hectares and under	458,120	55·23
From ½ to 1 hectares ...	85,921	10·36
,, 1 ,, 2 ,,	90,312	10·89
,, 2 ,, 3 ,,	50,576	6·10
,, 3 ,, 4 ,,	30,732	3·70
,, 4 ,, 5 ,,	20,213	5·91
,, 5 ,, 10 ,,	49,065	2·44
,, 10 ,, 20 ,,	28,151	3·39
,, 20 ,, 30 ,,	8,163	0·98
,, 30 ,, 40 ,,	3,187	0·38
,, 40 ,, 50 ,,	1,601	0·19
,, 50 ,, 100 ,,	2,661	0·32
Above 100 ,,	923	0·11
Totals	829,625	100·00

[1] A hectare is equal to 2·4711 acres.

Thus, out of the 829,625 occupations in 1895 more than half were 1¼ acres or less, and 86·28 per cent. were under 10 acres, as shown below :—

	Number of occupations
Half hectare or less	458,120
From ½ to 10 hectares	326,819
,, 10 ,, 50 ,, ...	41,102
Above 50 hectares	3,584
	829,625

It may further be explained that many of the smaller holdings near the cities are owned by men who go to work there, leaving their wives and families to look after the farm. Otherwise it would be impossible to live on them. The greatest proportion of the smaller holdings were in the Provinces of Western Flanders, Hainaut and Liége, which from an agricultural point of view are among the most prosperous parts of the country.

9. STATISTICAL.—Unfortunately no official returns are available showing the number of fowls kept in the country, nor yet the value of eggs and poultry produced. The last figures published was in 1866, when it was found that there were 4,500,000 poultry of all species, which, if all were adults, would not be much more than half a fowl per acre, about the same proportion as in Britain in 1885, and less than half as many as in Ireland, though the latter was based, not on the total area, but on the cultivated land. It is intended, I understand, to take another census at the end of 1910, and it will be very interesting to note the result. One great advantage of making the census on December 31 is that nearly the whole number of fowls recorded will be adult birds intended for breeding or laying stock. That there has been an enormous increase in the number of fowls kept since 1866 is unquestionable, but to what extent opinions differ greatly, and as these are estimated I do not give them, save in one instance, that of the Pays d'Alost, which is the great egg-producing section. The gentleman from whom I obtained these figures, M. de Mulder, will be referred to later, and knows the district thoroughly. He estimates that a million hens are kept for laying there, and that the total value of the eggs and poultry produced is 38,500,000 francs (£1,540,000) per annum. As, probably, Flanders accounts for nearly half

the total production of the country, it would appear that the annual value of the poultry crop is from 15s. to 20s. per acre of cultivated land in Belgium, which is a good, though not unduly high average, and could be equalled in Britain without any serious difficulty.

10. IMPROVED FERTILITY OF LAND.—Belgian farmers and cultivators of all grades realize the importance of supplying their land with those elements required for increasing its productiveness. Not a drop or particle of manure appears to be wasted. That poultry contribute greatly in this direction is recognized in all parts of the country, and it is acknowledged that the fertility of the soil has been raised considerably wherever fowls or ducks are kept. The facts given below are commended to the attention of our farmers, and especially to small and allotment holders. The most noticeable instance is met with in what is known as the Campine district, which extends from the city of Malines east and north to the Dutch frontier. At one period this was an arid sandy plain, covered with fir trees and incapable of cultivation. Some of it remains in the same condition, but considerable portions have been brought into use as market gardens. The story is deeply interesting and highly suggestive. About thirty years ago poultry-keeping was taken up by the peasants in this district on a somewhat extensive scale, primarily with the object of raising chickens for sale to the fatteners on the other side of Malines. The land was of little use for other purposes, and although there was not much natural food for the fowls in the soil, it was dry, the fir trees provided abundant shelter during the hot days of summer, and a moderate amount of insect life was obtainable. Eggs, also, were and are produced in large quantities throughout this district, though on such soil they are smaller in size and inferior in quality to those coming from hens kept on the richer lands. In the summer of 1897 I paid a visit to the district. Already a very marked change had taken place. The land near to Malines had been so enriched by manure from the poultry that it was capable of cultivation. For a distance of about five miles the trees were cleared and market gardens for production of asparagus and vegetables formed upon the old woodlands. At that time it was freely acknow-

ledged this result was largely due to the fowls, which were being bred in greater numbers all over the Campine country.

11. A CHANGED DISTRICT.—I was not, however, prepared for the developments which have taken place. At the time named (1897) we drove to Rymenam, Keerbergen, Putte, and Grasheide, through the fir woods, in which were cottages of a very humble type, attached to each of which were about 12 hectares (nearly 30 acres) of land, with very small clearances around the dwellings, little more than gardens. The people depended chiefly upon poultry-rearing for their incomes. At one place visited, a small inn, I was told that the owner had already (June) sold 350 birds, and had 400 more for disposal. In the previous year his sales of poultry amount to 4,000 francs (£160). At Grasheide we found a schoolhouse in the midst of fir woods, which came right up to the buildings on all sides. The teacher, M. Vanden Borchacht, reared about 4,000 chickens every year. Now the whole aspect is altered. As we drove in October last to the places named, it was to find the fir trees gone and the land under cultivation. Around the schoolhouse referred to has grown up a considerable village, in which a fine church is in course of erection. M. Vanden Borchacht is owner and principal of a large, well-built boarding-school opposite his old dwelling, and attributes his advance in life to the money made from poultry-breeding. What is true in his case is equally so in others, of which many examples could be given. Market gardens, grain and roots have taken the place of fir woods, owing to the improved fertility of the soil as a result of poultry kept thereon during a single generation. After the trees are removed it takes about two years to bring the ground into good condition, and, of course, it is capable of further improvement. Poultry are found everywhere. On most farms 300, 400, 500, or more chickens are bred every year. At one I was informed that 300 had been sold in a single day at 15 francs (12s.) per couple.

12. PROSPERITY FOLLOWS POULTRY.—Signs of prosperity are evident on all sides, both in the appearance of the people and their dwellings. Plate I. shows a farmhouse which I visited in 1907. Then it was a small thatched

cottage of a very modest size, which the nearer third with one chimney represents. A few years ago the owner was able to double the buildings, and recently a third portion, shown in the photograph with a higher roof, has been added, so that the dwelling and farm buildings are three times the size they were twelve and a half years ago. The capital expenditure is considerable, not provided by the landowner, but out of the earnings and savings of the farmer himself. This is but representative of what is met with over the entire district. The villages have grown considerably, the population has increased, and we have here an example which can be multiplied a thousandfold, not merely in Belgium, but elsewhere. A further sign of prosperity is seen in that whilst a dozen years ago dogs were almost exclusively employed for draught in the Campine country, horses are now used, and the roads are greatly improved. A more striking instance of the place occupied by poultry in respect to increasing the fertility of the soil and advancing the prosperity of the rural population I have not met with. Industry and thrift are necessary factors, and the people work hard. But for their labour is an abundant reward.

13. IMPORTS AND EXPORTS.—Whilst it is true that Belgium practically supplies her own requirements in respect to eggs and poultry, and has a small surplus for exportation, there is a fair amount of imports, as will be seen in the following figures, supplied to me by the courtesy of the Minister of Agriculture :—

BELGIAN IMPORTS AND EXPORTS FOR 1908.

			Imports			Exports
Eggs	{	Number ...	189,866,268	...	...	128,667,247
	{	Values ...	£573,490	...	...	£437,468
Live poultry ...	{	Kilogrammes	813,688	...	...	340,335
	{	Values ...	£61,866	...	...	£26,853
Dead poultry ...	{	Kilogrammes	42,028	...	...	546,320
	{	Values ...	£3,982	...	...	£49,348

From which it would appear that the balance of trade was £125,669 in favour of imports. It is recognized, however, that the figures as to imports are incomplete, as there are vast quantities of both eggs and poultry sent into France by road which are not included, and the estimate given to me is that were these recorded the balance would be on the other

PLATE I.—Improved Campine Farm Houses.
(Showing enlarged size as result of increased prosperity.)

PLATE II.—Straw Poultry House at Grashelde in the Campine.

side. In this connection it must be remembered that the above table does not include the eggs and poultry on transit through the country for shipment to British ports. According to the Trade and Navigation Returns for the year ending December 31, 1908, the imports of eggs and poultry were as follows :—

	Quantities				Values
Eggs	No. 255,611,200	...	...	...	£884,686
Poultry	—	...	...	...	£191,845
	Total value	...	...	...	... £1,076,531

Of these a very small percentage is Belgian, the bulk coming from Southern Europe. With respect to eggs imported, these are largely of cheaper grades to meet the demand for cooking purposes during the winter season, when Belgian eggs command as high prices as in England. Whether any foreign supplies are re-exported I was unable to learn, but in the period of great scarcity that is possible and probable. The live poultry imported includes the chickens brought from Italy, of which some particulars are given in the following chapter. It will be seen, therefore, that Belgium provides eggs and poultry more than sufficient to meet her own large demand for these two articles of food. That the country is capable of producing an increased quantity is evident, though in some districts the extension of market gardens, and of glass houses for fruit culture, may lead to reduction in the number of poultry kept. Should the industrial and commercial centres advance in extent and population as they have during the last two decades, with much greater needs and purchasing power, then there is little doubt that Belgium will be compelled to depend more and more upon extraneous supplies, and that the imports will advance considerably.

2

II.—METHODS OF HOUSING AND GENERAL MANAGEMENT.

14. SIMPLE METHODS.—The word which best describes the poultry industry of Belgium is simplicity. In spite of the fact that there has been a large increase in the number of fowls and ducks kept, with the exception of what may be regarded as fancy plants, whether owned by country and suburban residents or by artizans, the methods followed do not err on the side of elaboration. In many cases they are decidedly primitive as compared with those met with in the United Kingdom, America, Germany, and even Denmark. There is a total absence of whatever will add to labour without adequate recompense. It is for that reason incubators for a long period of time did not find acceptance; in fact, many peasants in the egg-producing districts do not believe in them, preferring the natural system of hatching. The great mass of Belgian farmers in many sections of the country would not accept an incubator as a gift if compelled to work it. They prefer to use hens both as sitters and mothers, even though they may not be able to hatch so early. But the best laying breeds are not brought out before May, when broody hens are usually available. This is not mere indisposition to change, but that they do not discard long-proved systems for the newest idea. As we shall see, however, in connection with table poultry, the use of incubators is becoming very general in the districts where flesh production is the main object, as there early hatching is all-important. As a rule, except in the last-named and the duck centres, the fowls are given freedom to wander, and if other classes of poultry are kept, no attempt to divide them is made, all mingling together. In fact, the opinion is held that ducks should always be kept with poultry, for they are said to purify the ground and prevent roup. What is the warrant for this view I am unable to state, and it is entirely antagonistic to that held elsewhere. It should not, however, be thought that the simplicity referred to is due to neglect, for that is not the case. Rather is the explanation to be

found in the avoidance of anything which adds to the cost of production, or to the increase of labour without gaining thereby. In many directions the Belgians are painstaking in the extreme, and give an amount of attention to detail which is praiseworthy in the extreme. Points which might be thought unimportant are attended to carefully. Examples of these are given in later chapters. But whenever by a little labour actual cash expenditure can be avoided that is freely given, and the money retained. Systems now adopted are in many cases those which have been followed for centuries. At the same time new ideas are making their influence felt, though the process is slow.

15. HOUSING.—In no direction is the conservatism of the Belgian peasants more evident than the question of housing. During my visits to the country, over many years, I have only met with one or two portable or separate poultry houses. In fact, there are probably more to be seen on the railway journey between Sevenoaks and Dover than in the whole of Belgium. Yet there are sections of the country where the provision of portable houses would be of the greatest service, enabling much larger numbers of birds to be kept without danger of disease, and distribute their manure over the land. Doubtless in process of time this development will take place, especially in the larger farm districts. The present system of housing restricts the numbers which can be kept with safety, for experience in all countries has shown that when the number of fowls kept is beyond the capacity of the land to utilize by plant growth the poultry manure produced then loss by disease is only a question of time. I feel convinced that the attacks of diphtheritis referred to in a later paragraph, attributed to the imports of Italian chickens, were to some extent due to increase of numbers without modification of method. Intensity of cultivation has, undoubtedly, done much to prevent any serious danger in many districts, but with the greater attention now paid to poultry and extension of the industry it will require to be kept in view, as must be the case everywhere.

16. FORMS OF POULTRY HOUSES.—In the vast majority of cases the poultry find accommodation in one of the farm

buildings, which may be either built of brick or stone, or a wooden structure. Except upon special plants few of these are satisfactory in respect to ventilation or light, contravening every hygienic principle, except that they are fairly clean. And in many cases they are evidently overcrowded, which is probably due to enhancing the number of fowls kept without increasing the accommodation. Places were visited where the fowl-houses were dark, with only a slit or opening in the wall for admission of fresh air, without any window, and at night when the inmates are on the roosts these must be veritable "black holes," with an atmosphere dense in the extreme. It speaks well for the vigour of the fowls that they are able to thrive under such conditions. But when it is remembered that great numbers of the dwelling houses, more especially on smaller farms, are built to conserve warmth by exclusion of air, it will be seen why poultry have to live under the conditions named, for we cannot expect that they will attain a standard above that of their owners. Moreover, as the birds get out very early in the morning, practically at break of day, they suffer less than would be the case if kept in for two or three hours longer. The only gain from this form of house is that, as a rule, they are cool in summer and warm in winter, though our experience is that an abundance of pure air and light are of supreme importance. There are signs, however, that the folly of such methods, and of over-crowding, is being realized, as some of the newer types of houses are improved in every way. Plate II. shows a house at Grasheide, in the Campine, made entirely of straw, almost like thatch, laid on to a wooden frame, and with an open front, which, it was stated, had proved most successful. Many of the quarters for poultry adjoin the stables, for the peasants believe that a connecting door into these is beneficial, but that poultry should never be kept near cows, probably more for the sake of the animals than of the birds. Perches are usually level, and nests are wooden boxes in tiers. In the Braekel country, with a view to the prevention of disease, slates are used in which a hole is pierced, large enough to permit the perch to pass through. These slates are placed sufficiently apart to allow space for one bird to roost, and they are fixed in position by a nail on either side. In this manner the birds are much cooler in summer than if sleeping close together, and parasites cannot pass from one to the other, as the slates are smooth and not limewashed. No special provision appears to be made for growing chickens save apportioning them a separate building. In some cases where a large number of birds are kept it is customary to make two such houses, using each on alternate months, and leaving vacant the other months, so that in turn each may be thoroughly ventilated and disinfected.

17. THE COLONY HOUSE SYSTEM.—So far as I was able to learn, no attempt has yet been made in the direction of what is known as the Colony House System, except, perhaps, to a slight extent in the table-poultry sections of Eastern Flanders. Taking into consideration the special conditions of the country and the intensification of production, this method should prove of the greatest benefit, and enable more poultry to be kept without the danger of disease, which arises as a result of increased numbers. In those sections of the country where land is cheap and population less in its density, such a system is not required, but on the richer lands it would have the dual benefit of enabling more birds to be kept and increasing the general crops.

18. HATCHING.—As indicated above, artificial methods of hatching have not been adopted generally. The official returns for 1895 show that at the time named there were only 505 incubators in the entire country, of which 20 per cent. were in Hainaut, probably in the hands of amateurs and fanciers. Since that time, as everywhere else, the number has increased manifold. Among the ordinary farms where egg production is the main object they are scarcely known, for the reason given in a previous paragraph—namely, that early hatching is not desired. Upon the duck farms of Laplaigne incubators are largely used, but in the Audenarde district hens are almost entirely employed. Here is a breed known as the Huttegem, a large fowl containing a considerable proportion of Bruges Game blood, which has been specially bred for development of the brooding instinct. They lay early, and when seven or eight eggs are produced commence to sit. They will cover nine or eleven duck eggs, and, what is more, will continue sitting for three months if

further eggs are given as soon as the previous lot is hatched. It is customary to sit several hens together, and when hatching takes place to give twenty-five to thirty ducklings to one hen and set the others again. She is not expected to cover, but only to keep them together and lead them where they can forage for themselves, though sometimes she is tied by the leg and not allowed to wander. In the table poultry districts, as previously mentioned, where early and prolonged hatching is necessary, incubators have been largely adopted. Throughout the Campine country, and around Londerzeel, Burgenhout, and Merchtem, even the smaller farmers possess these appliances. As a rule, they are either home or locally made, the metal parts, such as tank, regulator, and lamp, being sold by makers separately. I found that in the egg districts, such as Sottegem, Audenarde, and Renaix in Flanders, to the Herve tableland, natural hatching is the rule.

19. REARING.—It is unnecessary to enter into detail as to the methods adopted as to either hatching or rearing, as these are of the usual type, with few variations. The hens are set in one of the houses in open boxes or on shelves, and are lifted off for feeding. When the chicks appear they are cooped with the mothers in the open, the coops being of the simplest kind, in some cases straw on rods in apex form, the advantage of which is thought to be that as the straw is burnt when vacated by the brood, the risk of parasitic infection is greatly minimized. In other instances, wooden coops are employed. It is usual for the first few days to keep the broods close to the dwelling-house, so that they can be fed as often as required and looked after. Then they are put out in the open and allowed to wander at will. In the table-poultry districts artificial brooders are employed, and are to some extent indispensable, though even there, if a broody hen can be obtained, it is thought that better results follow the use of the natural method of rearing, especially as a hen can be trusted to lead the birds in search of food, and protect them against enemies, which the brooder cannot do. It will be seen, however, that at Lippeloo all the chickens are reared artificially, and that special provision is made for them. In the description of that interesting

establishment are given particulars as to the system, with illustrations of brooder-houses and brooder. Plate III. shows a brooder-house at Thimister, near Herve, in the province of Liége, which presents no special features. In it both sectional and individual brooders are in use.

20. FEEDING.—A Flemish proverb says: "Du cen hen houdfvoorhair ei is noy lotter als'ne kei" (He who keeps a hen for her eggs is like a round stone), which is simply a variation of the common old British saying that " Poultry don't pay." It is recognized that profit is dependent upon the limitation of cost in feeding, and that if all food is to be supplied where egg production is the main object, the expense will be greater than the return. The fact can scarcely be denied that in Britain and America there has existed and yet exists the idea that success can best be achieved by giving an abundance of food, with the result that there is no incentive on the part of the fowls to seek for natural supplies, that exercise in scratching is reduced, and laying checked by the fatty condition of body thus induced, and that the cost of production is greatly enhanced. Where fowls are feeding off, we desire to limit exercise and to increase the fatty deposits on the muscles, to which end food must be abundant, but that is only for a short period, at the end of which the birds are killed. It is an altogether different proposition with laying and breeding stock, for the fulfilment of whose functions the body must be lean. So far as I was able to learn, Belgian peasants do not err on the side of overfeeding, as no signs were apparent in that direction. In fact, where egg production is the principal aim, natural feeding is universal, and the birds find most of their own living on the fields, simply receiving once or twice per diem, according to the season of the year, a limited amount of grain. This explains, first, why the old ideas represented by the proverb quoted above have been abandoned to a large extent, and, secondly, why the industry is found so profitable on the basis of present-day prices for eggs. That the fowls thrive and lay well under such a system is acknowledged on all sides. I could not obtain any direct evidence as to the annual food cost of fowls on Belgian farms, because records are not kept, but the opinion

expressed was that this does not exceed 2s. to 2s. 6d. per hen per annum, which leaves a wide margin of profit between the expenditure and return.

21. SUPPLIED FOODS.—Apart from the natural food obtained by the birds, which varies in accordance with the districts and the quality of the soil, simplicity is found in this direction also, and cheapness is ever kept in view. For the rearing of chickens dari is largely employed, but for laying and breeding stock maize is the staple diet, by reason of its comparative cheapness, although it has risen greatly in price. Ten years ago this grain could be purchased at 8 to 9 francs per 100 kilos (2 cwt.) ; now it is 18 to 20 francs for the same weight, but every other food has also advanced. There can be no question that the low cost of this grain a few years ago encouraged poultry-keeping in Belgium, the result of which has continued. Fortunately, with the increased cost of food, there has been an equal advance in the prices realized for eggs, as a result of advancing demand. Belgian peasants have a strong belief in the value of buckwheat for poultry, but it is used by them to a very limited extent, as it is thought to be too dear. When soft food is given, chiefly during the winter season, rye meal is largely employed, mixed with Indian meal. It is one of the cheapest foods considering its digestibility and high nutritive value. Fowls do not care for the whole rye, and therefore it is always given after grinding. No ill-effects follow the use of maize, such as we have found in this country, owing to the fact that the birds are at liberty and keep in lean condition as a result of abundant exercise, and that the quantity supplied is small and supplemental to the natural food obtained. Something of this result is also attributable to the egg-producing breeds of Belgium being very active in habit and light in body, as shown in a succeeding chapter, and that they are less disposed to lay on internal fat than are heavier breeds. The winters on the Continent are more severe than in the United Kingdom, and, as a consequence, combustion of fat at that season is much more rapid. One interesting custom met with may be recorded. Where liquid is supplied in the shape of water, which is not often required, a little coffee is mixed with it, as that keeps it sweet for a consider-

PLATE III.—BROODER HOUSE AT THIMISTER (HERVE).

able period. Evidently the birds, whether old or young,
relish this mixture.

22. MILK SHEEP AND POULTRY.—As a result of the
increased cultivation of the country and fall in the price of
wool, the number of sheep kept in Belgium has been greatly
reduced. Official statistics record that in 1846 there were
662,508 of these animals, and in 1895 only 235,722. On the
smaller farms it is customary to keep two or three ewes for
the sake of their milk. It is stated that a good sheep will
yield as much milk as a goat, and they are not so troublesome. A further point is that they can be kept with hens in
considerable numbers and are not affected in any way, thriving
well on ground overrun by poultry. The opinion is very
general that cows and fowls do not go well together, but in
the Herve country, the great butter and cheese section of
Belgium, the poultry kept have increased greatly of late years,
and, so far as I could learn, without any ill-effects. The milk
from sheep is very rich indeed, and, as a good ewe will give
4 to 5 litres (7 to 8¾ pints) per day, they pay well. When
mixed with cows' milk for churning it gives firmness to the
butter. Further, the sheep are very valuable for eating off
the grass. Plate IV. shows some of these sheep in a poultry
run at Thimister, in the Province of Liége. Upon smaller
holdings in Britain it would appear that these sheep might
be introduced with advantage to the occupiers, especially in
districts where there is a short supply of milk.

III.—EGG PRODUCTION.

23. A GENERAL INDUSTRY.—Throughout the whole of Belgium the production of eggs is the main object of poultry-keepers. In a few districts, as shown in the succeeding chapter, specialization in one class or other of table poultry is met with, and the sale of surplus birds is at all times kept in view, notably in the borderlands of East Flanders and Antwerp, where the famous *poulets de Bruxelles* are raised extensively, in the Courtrai section of West Flanders, where the five-toed fowl of that name is found, in the duck-breeding districts of Audenarde and Laplaigne, and in Western Brabant, where the Ronquières turkey is bred. These, however, cover small areas. What are the comparative values of eggs and table poultry is unknown, but, from all the evidence obtainable, the former are several times greater than the latter. British imports of eggs are seven times larger in value than of table poultry, and production in the United Kingdom is probably three to one in favour of the egg. I am inclined to the view that in Belgium the disproportion is greater than with us. Whether on the sandy Campine, the richer lands of Flanders, the medium elevation of Brabant, the Herve tableland, or the hilly Ardennes, with the exceptions noted already, egg production is the main reason for poultry-keeping. In the chapter dealing with Belgian breeds will be found particulars as to the different races of poultry and their distribution. At one period poultry-keeping was largely confined to the lower-lying districts, where smaller farms are found. That is no longer the case. As mentioned above, on the uplands between Louvain and Liége, where occupations are greater in area, and in the Herve and other districts, poultry enter into the rural economy to an extent never known before. Changes, however, are taking place. One has already been mentioned. Another instance is seen in the rich district between Brussels and Namur, where around Ottignies fruit-growing under glass has developed enormously. Some of these may affect the poultry industry within small areas, but what is lost in one direction

will be gained in another. At one time there was a very common, but none the less erroneous, notion among English and Scotch farmers that poultry would injure growing corn or root crops. That, happily, is fast dying out, for it has been abundantly proved by practical experience that fowls clear the land of parasites and do not harm the plants, as well as add valuable manure to the soil. On the farms of Belgium they are accorded full liberty, and may be seen at work among crops of all kinds.

24. FARM WORK.—It has already been seen (para. 6) that poultry farms, with one or two exceptions, do not exist. Egg production is the business first and last of those to whom it is one of several branches. We do not find breeding centres such as have had great influence in the development of the Danish Poultry Industry, nor the great breeding plants, primarily for sale of stock birds and eggs for hatching, found in Britain and America, save where these are on fancy lines or for exhibition puposes. Without the former the great increase in Denmark could scarcely have taken place, for the poultry industry had to be built from the base. In the United Kingdom and America breeding plants as above referred to have *clientèle* at home or abroad not found elsewhere. A nation of poultry breeders, the Belgians have had for centuries at their disposal races of fowls, ducks, &c., eminently suited to the conditions of the country, with fixed characteristics and qualities highly developed. Tradition and experience and opportunity have equally favoured them. It is therefore essentially a part of the farm work and can only be extended as labour is available. Belgians have large families as a rule. Children are regarded as a source of riches. It is claimed that where there are many children the people are more industrious and thrifty, and that one or two children mean thriftlessness. The women or children look after the poultry, but the money all goes into one purse. Whether the man or woman sells the produce makes no difference. In the table-poultry sections it is the younger people with children who rear chickens, and the old people who keep hens for laying, as the labour with these is much less.

25. THE BRAEKEL COUNTRY.—What is known as the Pays d'Alost is the home of the most famous Belgian breed for

egg production. The district extends from Alost across the whole length of Flanders to the French border and beyond, in fact is almost co-extensive with the Flemish people—a rich, highly cultivated province, rich, that is in its soil, maintaining a large population, numbering in 1895, 2,306,582 people, rather more than 31 per cent. of the entire total. The figures given before (para. 8) will afford further information. Of this area East Flanders is the best productively, as the Escaut River and its tributaries flow through it towards the Scheldt. In West Flanders near the sea is reclaimed land not of much value. Of this great district Braekel and Nederbrækel form the centre. There and at Grammont, Sottegem, Audenarde and Reniax are the great egg markets. If appearances indicate the truth, the people are very prosperous. Without other sources of income they prove that agriculture is able to maintain in comfort a large, contented, and successful people, who with their simple tastes and habits are not only able to live, but can gather reserves for themselves and their children. One reason why egg production is the main object is that this is not a milk country, and therefore the best qualities of table poultry cannot be produced.

26. SOTTEGEM.—To avoid needless repetition three places are selected, for, whilst these present different features, they are each representative of others. Prior to the era of steam machinery the people around Sottegem were largely handloom weavers of linen, which was of exceptional quality. The factory system proved their ruin, as it has that of so many small rural industries. But this disaster has proved to be a blessing in disguise. It is said that formerly each peasant had so large a stock of linen that they had only one or two washing-days in the year, called the " great wash." As a result of the ruin of their industry they were compelled to depend upon the land, of which all had some share. Improvement rapidly took place. Production for sale went far beyond what was the case when merely for household requirements, due to the fact that now it is the source of, not supplemental to, livelihood. The farms are well cultivated, the towns and villages are prosperous in aspect, though by no means picturesque. Every farm has a flock of fowls, in some cases a fairly large one. The birds are well looked

after. Production is on an enormous scale, as will be seen below. The eggs are large in size and of very fine quality, due to the abundant and rich natural food obtained by the hens. There is a constant and good market in Sottegem for eggs, principally to meet the requirements of Brussels, which city is only 45 kilometres (about 28 miles) away, and with its more than half a million inhabitants provides a large and growing demand. A more striking piece of evidence of what can be accomplished upon small holdings under favourable conditions by skill, diligence, thrift, and enterprise, when combined with good markets for produce, has not come under my notice in any country. The last-named we have in Britain. Whether the former are possessed by our new occupants of the soil remains to be seen. I find that in 1895, of the land in Eastern Flanders 59·99 per cent. was in holdings of 1 hectare (2½ acres) and under.

27. BRAEKELS ON WATER MEADOWS.—On one side of Audenarde the conditions are similar to what may be found elsewhere in the Braekel country, and eggs are produced very largely. But in the valley of the Escaut, wherein the city stands, has been carried on for a very long period of time the rearing of ducklings, of which particulars are given in Chapter V. My present purpose, however, is to call attention to a change which is taking place, one that is very suggestive, and, if successful, may lead to a reconsideration of our ideas, both as to the places where chickens can be raised, and the food given to them. Reference should be made to the later chapter for details as to the water meadows which stretch from Audenarde itself up the broad valley for about 5 miles. During the last three or four years the number of ducklings has decreased, and that of chickens has increased. Many of the breeders who formerly kept only ducks, except a few hens for hatching purposes, now rear an equal number of each, permitting them all to run together on the meadows, which are entirely under water in the early part of the year, and are damp at other seasons. This change may be partly due to the fact that whilst the demand for ducklings is limited and does not grow rapidly, that for chickens and for eggs increases steadily and quickly. It is a strange sight to see the chickens running and seeking their food in the water

or ice, and the majority of poultry-keepers would expect that
great loss would arise by disease and death.   Mons. Vander
Snickt, writing in the *Illustrated Poultry Record*,[1] says that
" Chickens are said to thrive better on the wet meadows
than on dry fields where they must depend upon grain.   On
the meadows they find so large a quantity of animal food
along the ditches and in the moss that they do not touch any
grain.   It seems to me that the worms and insect food give
to the chicken feathers the same resistance to water as in
those of ducks.   On each farm about one hundred Braekels
are kept for laying and half a dozen Huttegems as brooders."
The question here raised demands investigation.   If chickens
can be raised successfully under such conditions, of course at
liberty—for in confinement the effect could not fail to be
disastrous—there are many sections of the country hitherto
believed to be unsuitable for fowls that could be utilized in a
profitable manner for poultry, and not of much value in other
directions.   Probably we should find that some of our breeds
would be less suitable than others for such conditions, though
it is acknowledged that the Braekel is not the most vigorous
race of fowls.   Also that chickens would do better than
laying or breeding stock on that class of ground, which is
confessedly cold in winter.   Further, a light-bodied, active
fowl would be less likely to suffer than one that is heavy and
lethargic.   It is, however, so novel and antagonistic to our
previous ideas that careful and comparative tests should be
made ere the system is adopted.

28.   RENAIX.—On both sides of the south-western frontier of Belgium and France the last generation has seen a
great development of industrialism, and a large accession to
the population engaged in the manufacture of cotton and
linen goods.   Lille and Roubaix in France, Tournai and
Courtrai in Belgium, are the centres of these respective districts.   In the small town of Renaix (called Rouse in
Flemish) are several flourishing factories, though it is in the
midst of a great agricultural country.   Increased demand
has led to an enormous development of poultry-keeping,
mainly for the production of eggs, and the Braekel fowl is

---

[1] October, 1909, p. 40.

everywhere, chiefly Silvers, though a few Golds and some Blacks are to be seen, the quality of which is very good indeed. The farms in this district vary in size, but the majority of them are about 10 hectares (24¾ acres). The number of poultry kept varies, depending to some extent upon the size of the occupation, though not wholly so. Flocks of 200 to 300 laying hens are to be found, but 80 to 100 are more general. As a rule, small farmers keep more in proportion to the acreage than those who have greater holdings. The result of the changes here noted are seen in a vast increase of production and general rise of prosperity. There is no question here as to whether poultry-keeping pays. The signs of prosperity are evident, and it is recognized on all sides that egg production has added greatly to the profits secured by agriculturists. The country around Renaix is very varied, with a good amount of hilly land and woods, on which fowls are seen everywhere.

29. TYPICAL EXAMPLES.—Two cases may be cited as representative of what is to be met with all over the district. These are a few miles out of Renaix. On one, a 10-hectare farm, about forty hens are kept, accommodated in the main buildings, but the roosting-place, which adjoins the stable, is dark and ill-ventilated, though kept very clean. It is evident that in this and many other places in Belgium I visited, the virtues of light and fresh air have not yet been realized, whether for human beings or live stock. The hens showed some signs of ill-effects from this cause, but were said to pay well. They have full liberty, and can find shelter in the ordinary farm-sheds if so disposed. The other farm was rather larger, very well kept, with good buildings and an excellently cultivated orchard. Here I found 110 layers, of which thirty were yearling pullets, very good indeed, all Silver Braekels, small in size of body, but well built for egg production. They were accommodated in a roomy building, distinctly above the average in respect to sanitation and ventilation. The custom is to keep no bird for more than three years, renewing part of the stock each season, at which age the. old hens are sold off. No other breed than the Silver Braekel is kept, as it is found that enough of the hens become broody to bring out the number of chickens

required, which is only about sixty or seventy per annum. From these the pullets are selected to fill the places of such old hens as are weeded out.

30. A BREEDING FARM.—M. Oscar Thomaes, who is a manufacturer at Renaix, has a breeding farm, called Villa des Poulets, a few miles out of the town, situated on high ground near extensive woods, by means of which he has been able to exert considerable influence upon poultry-breeding in the district. It is an excellently arranged place, part of which is divided into large runs for the breeding stock, the layers being kept in the farm buildings. Although it was a most unfavourable day when this place was visited, the character of the farm was evident. As a model estab-lishment demonstrating improved methods of breeding, housing and general management, it cannot fail to exert great influence. The breeds kept are Gold and Silver Braekels, Buff Orpingtons and Black Minorcas. M. Thomaes keeps Buff Orpingtons for winter laying, and by reason of the fact that brown-shelled eggs are preferred by some people, these selling for 1 centime more than those with white shells. A further point is that Orpington chickens are found to grow faster than Malines, and have not so much bone. As there is no fattening of poultry in the Renaix district, and the Orpington is fleshier than the Malines, although the latter are much the better at a later age and make greater weight when fatted, that is another recom-mendation. About 500 to 600 chickens are bred every year, all hatched and reared by hens. M. Thomaes distributes birds of improved quality to farmers in the district, buying chickens back from them in the autumn at 5 francs each, which he disposes of as breeding stock. This is profitable to the breeders, ensures improvement in the qualities of the race, and has been the means of greatly increasing produc-tion. Although M. Thomaes, who is President of the local Braekel Club, is an exhibitor, and has won a considerable number of prizes, his main interest is in development of practical poultry-keeping.

31. POULTRY ALLOTMENTS.—In another direction than large local demand there are many resemblances between

this section of Belgium and across the frontier in France, and the manufacturing districts of Lancashire and the West Riding of Yorkshire, where poultry-keeping by operatives has grown so enormously of late years. Renaix, which is a town of 22,000 inhabitants, may be taken as an example. Many of the artizans keep poultry on industrial lines, not merely for supply of their own households, but for sale of produce. These people live in the suburbs, where they are able to obtain 1 hectare (2½ acres) of land at an annual rental of 120 francs (£4 16s.), or, including a dwelling-house, at 200 francs (£8) per annum. In this respect they have an enormous advantage over North of England operatives, who, in many cases, have to pay an annual rent of £5 to £10 per acre without any dwelling, which is equal to £12 10s. to £25 per hectare. Consequently, as prices of eggs are quite as good around Renaix as in Lancashire and Yorkshire, and food costs no more, the Belgians can secure greater returns by their enterprise. I cannot but feel that the high rental of land in our manufacturing districts has seriously affected home production, and hope that by means of small holdings and allotments land may be obtainable on more equitable terms. In this direction small producers in Belgium are indeed favoured.

32. Axioms on Poultry-keeping. — Before leaving our consideration of egg production in the Braekel country there are several points which it will be well to place on record :—

Peasant poultry-breeders will never send a bird to an exhibition, or loan one for that purpose. They say it would be useless afterwards and might introduce disease.

As soon as a hen is three years old get rid of her, as she will not pay for her food. A hen four years old only lays three eggs and then rests. In selecting the best layers a question for enquiry is—how many eggs does a hen lay before taking a period of rest by ceasing to lay?

Peasants do not trap-nest. They handle both hens and ducks, and the egg can be felt if the bird will lay that day.

Braekels should never be hatched before May, though June is the better month. They mature rapidly, and if hatched early commence to lay too soon. June-hatched

3

pullets should begin to lay by October. That would not apply to other races.

Braekels rapidly succumb if attacked by disease, owing to the strain on the system by heavy egg production. An egg contains concentrated nutriment and drains the system unless properly fed. All prolific races have less power of resistance than such as are not subject to the same strain.

In the Pays d'Alost the soil is very rich and sticky, consequently the hens' feet get muddy and are liable to stain the nests and shells of eggs. To prevent that result, nests are placed at the back of the poultry-house, and the floor is littered with chaff or straw, which cleans the feet.

33. THE CAMPINE. — In the succeeding chapter one section of the Campine eountry is referred to—namely, where fowls are bred for table purposes. In Chapter I. (para. 10 to 12) the remarkable change in the district around Putte as a result of poultry-keeping has already been described. The greater part of the Province of Antwerp, together with a portion of Limburg, consists of a sandy plain, in which the soil is comparatively poor, having very little in the way of natural food supplies. In some districts there are fir woods, in others it is cleared and open. Here the conditions are entirely different from those met with in Flanders and other parts of Belgium. It is a great country for rabbits, which animals the peasants regard as we do rats, killing them off as far as possible, though these creatures breed so rapidly they appear to multiply quite as fast as they can be destroyed. As in other sections of the country, poultry-keeping has increased very greatly, chiefly, with the exception noted, for the production of eggs. This district is similar in many respects to the State of New Jersey in America in the nature of its soil. As I found in the State named, during 1906, poultry-keeping for the sake of eggs has grown very rapidly indeed. At one time the race of fowls kept was chiefly the Campine, of which particulars are given in Chapter VIII., but other breeds have been introduced and the Leghorn is now found very largely. On the plant owned by the Trappists referred to in the first chapter (para. 6) all are of that breed. Production is, however, very general. Every farm has its flock of fowls. Concentration

of supplies accounts for the enormous quantities sent to the City of Antwerp and elsewhere. But, as might be expected by the nature of the district, the eggs produced are smaller in size and lack the quality of those obtained from the richer lands. Methods followed are of the usual character, calling for no special description. One of the great hindrances to development of poultry-keeping, not only here but in other other parts of Belgium, is the losses from theft of the birds. It is not a question of foxes or other natural enemies, but human marauders. In spite of this, however, the industry has grown and is rapidly advancing.

34. THE HERVE COUNTRY.—Between the cities of Liége and Aix-la-Chapelle is the high tableland forming the frontier district towards Germany and the Maastricht corner of Holland, known as the Herve country. Although parts of it attain the elevation of 950 ft. above sea-level, and it is very cold indeed in winter, it is one of the most fertile sections of Belgium. There the finest butter and cheese are produced. The land is entirely pasture. At Herve, Battice and Aubel, all of which I visited, and whence magnificent views of the surrounding country were obtained, every field is cultivated, but not a foot of arable land could be seen. It maintains a large population. The signs of prosperity are evident on all hands. Thriving towns and villages, well-built and kept homesteads, and abundance of stock denote that the people find adequate reward for their labour. It is also a fruit district, where apple orchards abound. Unlike many parts of the Continent of Europe, hedges line the roads and divide the fields, affording shelter to the cattle, which, as in Denmark, are clad in rugs during the winter season owing to the low temperature which prevails. The soil is heavy but fertile.

35. EGG-FARMING.—Whilst it is true that the farms in this part of Belgium are as a rule small, they are perhaps a little above the average in size, though this is arrived at more by observation during my two visits to the Herve country than actual statistics. Until a few years ago poultry were kept mainly for domestic purposes, but there has been a large increase, and upon industrial lines, within the last five years.

Now they are to be seen upon almost every farm, frequently in considerable numbers. The general rule is that sixty to 100 laying hens are maintained, either around the homestead or in the orchards. These figures may be taken to represent the minimum, for 300 to 500 are by no means uncommon, and in one case a larger farmer has 1,000 head. I saw more separate poultry-houses in the Herve district than in the whole of the rest of Belgium, and it can fairly be anticipated that this system will extend rapidly, in order that the birds may be scattered over the land, which is desirable if tainted soil is to be avoided. With respect to the outbreaks of diphtheritis, referred to below, and from which this district has suffered to a considerable extent, I feel confident that the cause is to be found in the over-manuring of the soil and insufficient distribution of the fowls over the land. So far as I could learn the poultry does not affect the cows in any way, and that dairying and egg production can be conducted together. It may be hoped that, as separate houses are erected the open-front system may be tried even upon this exposed tableland. The methods of management adopted are, on the whole, very good, as the people here are progressive and intelligent. The majority of the fowls kept are Leghorns, which thrive excellently and give good results. Where care is taken these birds lay fairly well in winter, and it is stated that, by selection, in four years the average weight of eggs produced in the district has been increased by 8 grm. (rather more than $\frac{1}{4}$ oz.). The average weight is from 50 to 60 grm. ($1\frac{7}{8}$ oz. to $2\frac{1}{8}$ oz.), which is below those produced in Flanders. There is a breed peculiar to this district, known as the Herve, mentioned in Chapter VIII., and efforts are being made to improve and popularize it. The Brackel and Campine fowls are too delicate, and the Malines fowl suffers from rheumatism on this heavy soil.

36. ITALIAN FOWLS AS LAYERS.—About fifteen years ago a trade was introduced which has had a vast influence on the development of poultry-keeping in Belgium, more especially in those districts where production at the time named was on a small scale. This was the importation of chickens from Italy when about 10 weeks old, weighing about 2 lb. each. These were sold to the farmers, who kept them as layers for one

season, selling in the following summer, when a fresh lot was purchased. These birds were brought over from Northern Italy, in crates holding thirty, of which two were cockerels and twenty-eight pullets, and were all of Leghorn type, but very varied in colour. The cost of carriage amounted to 3d. per bird, and they were sold in Belgium at about 2 francs each. The trade grew enormously. In one year about 600,000 were imported. The pullets proved to be splendid layers, and were hardier than the native races. M. Vander Snickt suggests that the transference of a fowl from South to North tends to stimulation of egg production, whilst change from North to South induces fattening, the former of which is confirmed in Belgian experience. These Italian fowls gave a vast impetus to poultry-keeping in Belgium. Farmers in all parts of the country bought supplies and made money out of the business. The gain thus secured has never been lost, and it is estimated that three times as many eggs are produced than was the case fifteen years ago. It was not, however, all gain. In Italy, owing to the bad methods followed by breeders, there has been a great amount of disease among poultry, as I saw during my visit to that country nearly six years ago. The system of transit developed latent sickness, and diphtheritis was introduced, causing immense loss to Belgian poultry-keepers. In many cases the imported birds survived and recovered, whereas the native birds died off if attacked. The trade has greatly declined, and comparatively few are now imported. Leghorns seen in Belgium are chiefly descended from those brought over in previous years. The Minorca, introduced from England about ten years ago by exhibitors, has largely displaced the Leghorn over a large area in the Provinces of Liége and Namur.

37. SIZE AND COLOUR OF EGGS.—The difference in size of eggs produced in Flanders and on the Campine respectively has already been mentioned. The former are the largest in the country, those from hens often reaching an average of $2\frac{1}{2}$ oz. each, whilst $2\frac{3}{4}$ oz. eggs are by no means uncommon. I was informed by a large Brussels merchant that eggs from the Braekel country average 60 grammes, which is nearly 17 lb. per 120. From the Campine they are smaller, as well as

such as are produced around Liége. Wavre is a great market for eggs, as many as half a million having been sold on a single day, but here again they are smaller than in Flanders. Yet the standard of size for the whole country is very good, distinctly higher than that of Britain. Whether this is due to the conditions or to selection cannot be stated definitely. Probably both influences have shared in the result. Braekel eggs have always been large in size, but when I first knew the Campine nearly 25 years ago the eggs from that breed were distinctly smaller than is the caso now. The increase has been partly due to crossing with the Braekel, but mainly to selection of larger-sized eggs for hatching. In a previous paragraph (35) is recorded what has been accomplished in the Herve district. So far as colour of shell is concerned, the majority of Belgian breeds produce white-shelled eggs, but there are a few minor exceptions which are bred to a very limited extent. The Orpington is rapidly advancing in several districts, and coloured-shelled eggs are regarded with favour. At Brussels, Liége, and Renaix I learnt that they command, wholesale, one centime more than those with white shells. This is not much, but it represents 10 francs per thousand. It is well known that coloured shells are stronger than white ; they carry and keep better. Some pastry-cooks state that they can get the same result from two brown-shelled eggs as with three white ones, and restaurateurs think the flavour is finer. Upon these latter points definite evidence is wanting. The claim is made, however, that eighteen Braekel eggs give equal results in cake-making to twenty-two from any other breed.

38. AVERAGE PRODUCTION.—The Braekel and the Campine fowls have always been famous as layers, which is equally true of their first cousins, the Hamburghs, though the eggs of the latter are much smaller in size. Claims have been made that they produce 300 eggs per annum, but this is an exaggeration, probably caused by the performance of one hen out of a million. From such evidence as I was able to obtain a very common flock average is 150, some of the hens reaching a total of 200 in the first year, and others corre. spondingly fewer. That breeders keep this all-important question in view is certain. There is, however, nothing like

the systems of recording which I found at Danish breeding centres in 1907, with selection of the best layers for stock purposes. The absence of actual records makes statements somewhat doubtful. Still it may be accepted that fecundity of Belgian hens is high, as the peasants have short shrift for the bad layer.

39. PRICE OF EGGS.—Demand in the Lille district of France determines the price of eggs, at any rate in the western provinces of Belgium. Competition between that city and Brussels for supplies is very keen. The country is so small and consuming centres so near that trading rings cannot prosper. The result is that prices are high and well maintained. At the end of October I found, at Sottegem, producers were receiving in the open market 1s. 4d. to 1s. 6d. per dozen for their eggs, and at Renaix 1s. 6d. to 1s. 7d. per dozen. The lowest price in the spring does not fall below 8 centimes (9½d.) per dozen, and in winter it goes up to 20 centimes (2s. per dozen), so that prices are quite as good as in England. There may be sections of the country where rates are lower, but I did not hear of them. Even in Liége, where the eggs are not so large, returns were nearly as high as those quoted.

40. WINTER SUPPLIES.—As previously mentioned (para. 13), a considerable quantity of cheaper grade eggs are imported for cooking purposes during the winter season, principally from southern Europe. The Belgians have, however, done much to increase production at that period of the year when prices are at their highest. I was interested to see the quantities sold in the various markets visited ; small as compared with what are brought in during the spring and summer, but showing a very satisfactory proportion. For instance, at Sottegem, on the day that market was visited (October 20th), 150 hampers, holding 1,000 eggs, were dispatched by rail. In April the maximum of 450 such hampers is reached. A 1-to-3 proportion is very good indeed. Similar evidence was obtained elsewhere, varying somewhat in accordance with the district. This satisfactory result has been attained by careful management and by breeding the pullets so that they

commence to lay in September and October. At Renaix, although the adult hens were not through the moult, pullets were producing freely. The Belgians say that they can bring the birds into profit during the autumn by making them find all their own food for a fortnight, the exercise of scratching consuming the reserves of fat, and then feeding upon steeped oats, which method I first heard of in Russia a few years ago. It is evident, therefore, that the advance in supplies of eggs during the winter season is not due to any climatic advantages, for such are not present, over those found in Britain, but to regulation of the time of hatching pullets in accordance with the period of growth of each respective breed, so that they may begin laying in September and October. It must be remembered that the great Belgian egg-producing races are small in size of body and attain maturity with great rapidity, whereas our breeders have gone in for larger fowls, and have even increased the weight of some of our best laying races merely for the show pen. I have often pointed out that this is fatal to increased prolificacy and winter egg production. To English breeders the Braekel and Campine look weedy and small, but the Belgian knows that it is folly to expect that a heavy milker or layer will be as large or as fleshy as a beef or flesh producer.

PLATE   ...TENING ROOM AND CAGES.

IV.—MARKET POULTRY.

41. An Old Pursuit. — For how many centuries Belgium has been celebrated for the quality of its table poultry it is impossible to state. The records have not been discovered, if ever made. We may assume without risk that for hundreds of years Flemish people have been skilled at this work, as they are to-day. The fourteenth and fifteenth centuries were periods of great prosperity in the Netherlands, and at that time fattening was general for production of high-quality poultry consumed by the nobility and wealthy citizens. Now the demand is vastly greater than ever before. Not only does Belgium provide for her own needs in this respect, which are very large, as it is stated that more than a million fowls are sold in Brussels every year, and does not import, but she sends large quantities to France and Germany, of which more is said below. Some time ago when visiting the City of Lille I saw large numbers of good quality fowls named "Bresse," shaped in the manner met with in the Bresse section of France, and on inquiry learnt that these were almost exclusively Belgian. In fact, a considerable proportion of the birds consumed in the Lille district, as of the eggs, are brought from Flanders.

42. Poulets de Lait.—The trade in table fowls resolves itself into three branches. First, is that in *poulets de lait*, or milk chickens, the sale of which is very large indeed during the early months of the year. These little birds are a great delicacy. They are produced exclusively in the egg districts, as those races which are used for larger table poultry are useless for this purpose. It will be remembered that in my American Report[1] the fact was recorded that the squab boilers, as they are called, are largely produced from the laying breeds of poultry, such as the Leghorn. American birds are larger than the Belgian, which latter are killed when eight weeks old, weighing 8 to 10 oz., at which

---

[1] Report on the Poultry Industry in America, 1906, pp., 80-81.

age they are naturally in fleshy condition without any
special preparation, except that for about two weeks the
birds selected for killing are fed upon soft food mixed with
milk, which softens and whitens the flesh.   They are, in
fact, the cockerels of light-bodied, egg-producing breeds,
which will never again, if permitted to grow, have much
value for table purposes.   At the age named they realize
2 francs each, whereas at twelve weeks old they will not be
worth more than 70 centimes.   The finest *poulets de lait* are
Braekels, Campines standing next, with Leghorns a bad third
in rank.   It is, therefore, in Flanders chiefly where the
peasants reap considerable advantage by the sale of the
cockerels in this manner.   One reason why the breeds named
are preferred is their rapid development, and that the sex
can be distinguished by the comb much earlier than is the
case with heavier races.   The point to be emphasized in this
connection is that the production of *poulets de lait* is not a
special industry, but is combined with the breeding of pullets
for egg production, and that profits are greatly enhanced by
the sale of birds which otherwise would be costly to feed and
realize low prices.   The fact is understood throughout nearly
all the egg districts visited, where poultry-keepers of all
grades turn the cockerels into money as rapidly as possible.
A large English egg-producer once said that if he could
distinguish the sex when the chickens were hatched, he
would wring the neck of every cockerel.   But it is better to
turn them into money.   As already mentioned (para. 6), an
attempt was made some time ago to raise these baby chickens
on a wholesale scale, but it was not financially successful, and
the right breed was not selected.

43. POULETS DES GRAINS.—These form the second class,
and are similar in all respects to our spring or asparagus
chickens.   Production, however, is not so general as that of
the smaller birds, as the Braekel and other races of that type
are of little use for this purpose.   One reason for the growing
popularity of the Buff and White Orpingtons is that these
mature more rapidly than the Malines fowl, and can be
killed at 3½ months old, without need of fattening, when
they are in plump, meaty condition.   Malines, however, and
other fowls of that type are frequently used.   In this case,

also, the birds are not subjected to fattening, but are fed off for a couple of weeks on food into which a large amount of milk enters, buttermilk chiefly. As a rule, this class of poultry are killed when weighing 2 to 3 lb., for which prices are good, ranging from 4 to 6 francs.

44. POULETS DE BRUXELLES.—During the summer, autumn, and winter an enormous trade is done in large fowls, which form the stable production in several districts as described below, and in which there is a large and growing trade with France and Germany. Within a small portion of East Flanders, between the cities of Malines and Termonde, is to be found the great table-poultry district of Belgium, resembling to some extent Sussex and West Kent though the area is smaller, but the work is carried out on more intensive lines, so far as the rearing is concerned. The fowl used for this purpose is the Malines almost exclusively, producing birds large in size, soft in bone, and carrying a great amount of beautifully white flesh. In five to six months these birds will weigh 8 to 10 lb., and about Christmas a little more. These sell at from $1\frac{1}{2}$ to 2 francs per lb. wholesale, for the best specimens. The appearance when seen in the markets or poulterers' shops is not attractive, in that the breast is crushed almost flat, and as they are killed by cutting the throat, a great gash is evident. Bleeding whitens the flesh, but the French method of paletting is preferable, as it does not spoil the look, though probably less humane. Some years ago M. Vander Snickt endeavoured to encourage a trade with London for *poulets de Bruxelles*, but the English refused to have birds flattened, and as Belgian fatteners would not then alter their method (though they have since been compelled to do so for the German trade), saying it was their trade mark, the project fell to the ground. Surely producers should meet the requirements of their customers in questions of this kind. Whilst Belgian table poultry is excellent in quality, it does not excel, even if it equals, the finest grades of English, except for the very largest winter fowls, which are, in my judgment, superior to ours, due partly to the breed and partly to the system of rearing and fattening.

45. THE TABLE-POULTRY AREA.—For a long period
of time the production of poultry for market has been an
important industry in the district of which Malines, Puers,
Termonde, and Alost form the border line. This includes
the small towns or villages of Londerzeel, Burgenhout,
Lebbeke, Opwyck, and Merchtem—a country bordering on
one side the Campine where the soil is sandy, but as a rule
is good though not so rich as further West. It is, however,
well cultivated and very prosperous, largely owing to the
breeding of poultry. Cows are kept extensively for butter,
which fact explains why the production of table poultry has
grown to so great an extent. In fact, one influences the
other. Success in fattening depends chiefly upon the use
of buttermilk, which is employed as is soured skim milk in
England. I was told again and again that more fowls
would be fattened if a larger supply of buttermilk were
available. The number put up is determined by the quantity
of that product available. Demand has enhanced the price.
At one time it could be bought for 2 centimes the litre, now
it is 6 centimes. Since my previous visit to this district the
industry has grown enormously, and is now of large dimen-
sions and influence.

46. LONDERZEEL.—The little town of Londerzeel for a
long period has been a great market at which rearers and
fatteners have met, the one to sell, the other to purchase,
birds. I remember years ago seeing the constant stream of
dog-drawn carts laden with crates of fowls *en route* to that
place, brought from villages 10 to 20 miles away, and the
same was true at Merchtem. Then comparatively little was
done in rearing near at hand, and the supplies were drawn
from a wide area. Londerzeel was primarily a centre for
fattening. But a great change has taken place, and as it is
representative of the entire district named, what is stated
respecting it may be applied to Burgenhout, Merchtem, and
Lebbeke. M. Joseph Plaskie, to whose courtesy I am greatly
indebted, states that ten years ago not more than 500 birds
were annually reared in the commune of Londerzeel, which
embraces 1,800 hectares, and has a population of 2,000.
Now it is not unusual to find 50,000 chickens at one time.
Every one breeds poultry, farmers and those with even a

small plot of land, but the number in each individual case is generally small. He estimates that 200 breeders of first quality birds in this neighbourhood produce 10,000 chickens annually, and that 300 smaller occupiers rear 5,000. A little further afield the farmers individually rear larger numbers. In some cases people with not more than 6 ares of land (about ½ of an acre) rear 1,000 chickens every year. There are 25 to 30 fatteners at Londerzeel, who kill, three times per week, 100 to 150 birds each in the busy season, averaging all the year round 60 to 80 per day. From this centre about a million francs worth (£40,000) are sent to Brussels by road, whilst for several months of the year 500 to 600 are despatched daily to Germany. Great prosperity has followed the extension of poultry breeding and fattening all over the district, in which every section of the community has shared, and some people have made modest competencies out of it. The satisfactory feature is the dissemination of benefits. Rearers, whether farmers or small occupiers, have reaped the advantage. A large proportion of the supplies are obtained from the Campine country, on the other side of Malines, and are usually purchased in the market of that city. These come from the district referred to in paragraphs 10 to 12, where the improved fertility of the land as a result of poultry-keeping has been so remarkable. The Campine-reared chickens, however, are not so fine in quality as those produced in the Londerzeel district, as might be expected by the nature of the respective soils. But a great improvement has taken place in the Campine birds, due to the change in the nature of the land.

47. METHODS ADOPTED.—Practically speaking, all the fowls bred are Malines; in the Londerzeel district single-combed, in the Campine Turkey-headed. The majority of farmers and small occupiers keep their own stock birds, and rear the chickens until they are ready for the fatteners. Under these circumstances from 20 to 50 hens are maintained at each place with the necessary males. There are, however, other systems in vogue. Breeding farms are increasing in number, which supply eggs for hatching at fixed prices. Some of the fatteners send out newly-hatched chickens for rearing at farms, supply all food, and pay 25

centimes per bird when taken away, which seems very little
indeed, but the peasants regard the value of manure obtained
in this way at 1 franc the couple, and are quite contented
with the arrangement. M. Plaskie has four incubators at
work, from which he supplies chickens and all food, paying
1 franc each for the labour of rearing. In some cases he
provides half the food and takes half the chickens. Old hens
from this district at the end of the breeding season are sent
to Antwerp and Brussels for sale to the Jews and realise
3 to 4 francs each.

48. HATCHING AND REARING.—Belgian peasants have
been very slow in adopting artificial methods of hatching and
rearing, and, as we have already recorded, incubators are
very seldom found in the egg-producing districts. That is
not, however, the case in the Londerzeel area, where the
necessity for early and prolonged hatching has made imperative the use of these appliances, which are now very largely
employed. It is found more profitable to keep the hens in
lay than to use them for brooding. Many farmers possess
one or more incubators, and where the chickens are supplied
either by fatteners or others they are generally hatched artificially. In this respect a very great change has taken place
within recent years, and a considerable proportion of the
chickens are brought out by incubators. In fact, I do not see
how it could be otherwise. The present development would
have been impossible by natural methods alone. The incubators used are, as a rule, made locally by carpenters, who
purchase the metal and regulating parts, to which they add
the wood-work required. Both tank and hot-air machines
are used, the former predominating. I was unable to obtain
authoritative records as to results, but these are regarded as
satisfactory. So far as rearing is concerned, both hens and
brooders are employed. Only one point need be mentioned,
namely, that the use of glasshouses for rearing in the early
stages is growing. These are practically greenhouses, 6ft. to
7ft. high, roomy and well ventilated, in which the brooders
are placed, wherein the inmates are protected against cold and
wet, and obtain all the sunshine available—a most important
consideration in the colder months of the year for rearing
chickens, especially those intended for killing. The system

is one of forcing growth, but that is desirable. Glass fronted brooder houses are now used in Britian and America, and all glass-buildings deserve a trial for intensive rearing. Soft food is largely used for the birds at this stage. So far as I could learn dry and hopper feeding have not been introduced.

49. A NOTE OF WARNING.—Experience in many countries has abundantly proved that with greater numbers the risks of loss by disease becomes a serious factor. As already explained (para. 15), when the animal life is in excess of the capacity of the soil to utilize the manure produced, sooner or later disease will break out. In some of the places visited I felt that hygienic conditions were absent, equally on farms and small holdings ; at the former by keeping the birds around the homestead in such numbers instead of distributing over the land, at the latter by overcrowding in small runs. In a few instances the ground is only utilized for one season, and afterwards cultivated, other plots being used in succeeding years. But this method will have to be systematized to a greater extent than is now the case. A few months ago a sharp lesson was received by a serious outbreak of diphtheritis in the district, which occasioned great loss, due entirely to overcrowding and the neglect of hygienic principles, which, it may be hoped, will emphasize the importance of this question. I am also certain that the present system of breeding from young pullets to secure early eggs, hatched artificially, will lead to reduced vigour of the stock, and that, whilst for birds to be killed early such a system is necessary, it is essential that those which are intended as breeders should be hatched and reared naturally and not forced. To that all-important point at present a very small amount of attention has been given.

50. FATTENING ESTABLISHMENTS. — In the great majority of cases, as in Sussex, breeders do not fatten and fatteners do not breed, at least in so far as the larger establishments are concerned. A few of the latter send out birds to be reared, as mentioned above (para. 47), keeping the breeding stock themselves. A fair number of farmers fatten their own poultry, but the tendency is to division of labour in the way indicated, the benefits of which are obvious, as profits are thus widely distributed. So great is the demand

for birds that fatteners are compelled to pay high prices to secure supplies.   Competition is all in favour of breeders. The birds are usually purchased by fatteners in Londerzeel, Malines and other markets, and are not, as a rule, collected from the individual farms.   As might be expected, there is much difference in the way in which the work is carried out. At some of the places visited the methods were excellent, at others capable of considerable improvement, more especially as to cleanliness.   Generally speaking, the sheds and cages are thoroughly cleaned every time a fresh lot of birds is put in.   The manure is not removed during the process, but covered up, as disturbance is thought undesirable by reason of the ammonia given off.   "Manure is gold;" every particle is conserved and utilized on the land.   Plate V. shows the exterior of the sheds owned by M. Louis Kizmotin, at Londerzeel, entered from a yard behind his house.   These sheds are in the permanent buildings and occupy several rooms, of which it was impossible to secure satisfactory photographs.   At this place, which is very well managed, about 1,000 birds were in the cages, and those dead showed very high quality.   One of the best establishments visited was that of M. Koorman, of Burgenhout, having two floors with cement between, excellently arranged and well managed, and where more attention is paid to ventilation than in the majority of cases.   At many places special brick buildings have been erected.   As a rule these are divided so that not more than 200 birds are in one room.   One thing I was sorry to see, namely, that some of the fatteners are also inn-keepers, as that tends to the encouragement of drinking. Plate VI. shows the method of caging.   Cages are usually in two rows, one behind and higher than the other, but not above, so that the manure falls directly to the ground.   As a rule the rooms are not well lighted, but the value of fresh air is theoretically recognized, though not practised to the same extent.   Warmth is believed to be an essential factor, and in winter the roof is lined with straw, but that is removed during the warmer months, as it would be a harbourage for parasites.

51. NO CRAMMING.—The period of feeding is from three to five weeks, depending upon the size of the birds

|PLATE VII.—A BELGIAN CARPENTER'S FLOCK OF MALINES.

T Brooder House at Lippeloo.
ns are kept for the first month.)

and the time of year. In that period the birds will increase in weight by ½ kilo (1¼ lb.) or more. It is found that the larger fowls when put up to fatten do not proportionally increase in weight to the same extent as do smaller specimens, the chief benefit being in softening the flesh by adding fat to the muscles. The great differences between English and Belgian systems of fattening are that in Belgium the fowls are placed in the sheds from the first and kept there all the time, not for half the period as with us, and that they are trough-fed all that time, and not crammed during the latter half of the process. Cramming is not adopted as in England and France. I found a strong disbelief in the advantages of cramming throughout Belgium, perhaps because those who have tested the system were not skilled at the work and did not obtain the best results. It may be, also, that for the *poulets de Bruxelles*, which are usually 5 to 8 months old when killed, equal results are not obtained as with younger birds, though that is not so in France. The fact, however, is as stated, namely—that cramming is not used in the production of Belgian table poultry, which are entirely trough-fed. My opinion is that Belgian fowls, with the exception of *poulets de lait*, lack the fulness of skin and finish of the best qualities of the English and French, by reason of the fact that they are not crammed. I should be glad if we could discover a method by which the same results could be arrived at by trough-feeding, and thus dispense with cramming, but that has not been reached as yet.

52. FEEDING AND KILLING.—The staple food given during this period consists of buckwheat meal and buttermilk. Sometimes the former is varied by the addition of a little maize meal, but that does not give the same results in colour and flavour of the flesh. No fat is added to the mixture, as there is sufficient in the buttermilk, which is the most important part of the food, and is richer than the soured skim milk used in Sussex. In fact, as already seen, the extension of fattening is determined by the supply of this product, which has risen greatly in value. The mixture named is given thin at first and thicker later, and is fed twice or thrice a day from the troughs suspended in front. As soon as the birds are satisfied all remaining is removed. When ready for

killing, the fowls are starved for twenty-four hours to empty
the crop and intestines, but if any food is found therein it is
removed by a spoon.   Killing is by cutting the throat, and
plucking takes place as soon as the blood ceases to flow,
whilst the body is warm.   Men are usually employed on the
larger plants for this work, and earn not more than 3 to
4 francs per day.   At others the members of the family all
take part in it.   When denuded of feathers the birds have
the sternum crushed in by blows from a mallet for the home
trade, and are laid on boards, breast downwards, to cool.
In summer they are usually finger drawn.   So far as I was
able to learn, at no place is ice used for chilling, but that is
equally true in Sussex, though the benefit would be very
great.   When sent away the fowls are usually graded and
packed in hampers holding fifteen each.   The cost of fattening is stated to be 60 centimes to 70 centimes (6d. to 7d.)
each.

53.   POULTRY FARM AT LIPPELOO.—About a mile from
Malderen Station in the same district is the Château de Melis,
at Lippeloo, the property and residence of the Vicomte
Edmond de Beughem, where is what has been described as
the only poultry farm in Belgium, and which has special
features of great interest.   It is an old Flemish château of the
sixteenth century, surrounded by water, with great courtyard
and the usual buildings.   Practically in the Campine country,
though much of the land has been cleared, fir woods are
found on two sides.   The system adopted is original.   Every
autumn about 600 Malines pullets are selected as breeding
stock, which, with the necessary male birds, are loaned to
farmers and others in the district, each flock numbering
thirty to fifty in accordance with the accommodation available.   These remain the property of the Vicomte, who
takes them away the following autumn and replaces by a
new flock.   The lessees, to use a legal term, provide the food
and look after the birds, sending in to the château twice a
week all the eggs obtained, for which they are paid from
10 centimes (1d.) to 18 centimes each, according to the
season of the year.   It is estimated that in this way they
can make a profit of 7 francs (6s. 6d.) per annum from each
hen, which from their point of view must be satisfactory,

considering that they have not the expense of purchasing or of rearing the breeding stock. Plate VII. represents a flock of forty fowls held under this system by a carpenter at Lippeloo, and who informed me that last year he had made a profit of nearly 300 francs (£12). At the time of my visit, early in November, he was bringing in about 100 eggs per week.

54. HATCHING AT LIPPELOO.—As the eggs are received they are stamped with the sender's name, to check fertility, by M. Feyaerts, the energetic and skilful manager, who, as a resident for seven years in England, is well acquainted with our methods. As something like 20,000 eggs are handled every season the importance of some such check is apparent. All are hatched by incubators. In one of the permanent buildings two rooms are devoted to this purpose, in each of which are eight machines, holding 250 eggs, so that the total hatching capacity is 4,000 eggs. The rooms are airy and spacious, lighted on the east side, and having thick brick walls are very equable in temperature. Arrangements for ventilation might be improved, though not bad. The incubators are made at Lippeloo, and have a double action, not only raising the second chimney cap, but opening ventilators above the pipes which are used instead of a tank, causing them to cool rapidly. Regulation is obtained by ether and mercury in a circular glass tube fixed to a disk of wood, which moves on a central pivot as the heat rises or falls, and thus operates the regulator. Water trays are placed below the egg drawers. I was informed that these machines give excellent results, and the conditions are certainly favourable.

55. BROODER HOUSES.—For the earlier stages of rearing, two long range houses, built of brick, are employed. The first of these is 150 ft. long by 12 ft. deep, and 8 ft. high in front, which is glass-fronted. It has an excellent system of ventilation behind and in front, and is warmed by means of steam pipes running along the back wall. Plate VIII. shows the outside of this building, the weakness of which is that the runs outside are inadequate as compared with the number of chickens kept, and, unfortunately, cannot be extended. This is a very common mistake, and I have

met with many instances of the same nature both at home
and abroad, in America as well as in Europe.   All that can
possibly be devised has been done to keep the ground sweet
by planting fruit trees and vegetables, and up to the present
there has been no disease.   In fact, the mortality has not
exceeded 7 per cent. per annum, which is very good indeed,
but the enterprise is only five years old, and the full effects
of this system have not yet been reached.   A ¼ acre of land
for a house holding nearly 4,000 chickens, even though that
is only for the first month, is totally inadequate.   Had there
been eight times as much it would not have been too great.
This is the danger of permanent brooder houses, which
should always have plenty of ground space outside.   Into
this house the chickens are brought from the incubators
and accommodated in large, round, wooden brooders
(Plate IX), which are 6 ft. in diameter and 2 ft. high.
Inside each brooder is a circular metal water tank about
6 in. wide, resting on iron stands, and with a large space
in the centre.   On top is a large wooden cover with a
central window which is movable for ventilation and inspection, in addition to which are air-holes all round the sides,
and pipes in the lid.   Fifteen of these brooders are used,
each accommodating 250 chickens.   Although it is stated
that the result is satisfactory, I cannot but think that more
sub-division of numbers would be better.   At first the heat
is maintained at 85° F., and gradually reduced to 68° F., by
the time the chicks are a month old, when they are able to
dispense altogether with artificial heat, and are transferred
to the second house.   This is 180 ft. long by 18 ft. deep
9 ft. high at one side, falling to 6 ft. at the other.   At the
end nearest the main building are a food store and room for
heating apparatus, as shown in Plate X.   The house is well
lighted on both sides and can be heated when required by
hot-water pipes, which is only needed during very cold
weather.   The system of ventilation is excellent.   The pipes
are against the west wall, behind which are inlets for air,
and in front is a broad wooden screen about 2 ft. high, thus
carrying fresh air during the entire length above the heads
of the chickens, which sleep on low movable laths or
perches.   As the air must pass over the pipes, when these
are heated it is warmed.   The floor in both houses is made

of fine ashes and chalk mixed and moistened, so that
it can be bedded down hard, presenting a smooth, even
surface, easily cleaned. It is dry but warm. Both back
and front of this house are runs for winter and summer
respectively.

56. RUNS FOR GROWING BIRDS.—When the chickens
are six to eight weeks old, in accordance with the season of
the year, a second transference takes place, this time to open
runs in the fir woods, where the trees have been partly
cleared, as shown in Plate XI. These enclosures are about
a quarter of an acre, and as each flock consists of about
150 chickens, this gives about 30 sq. ft. for every inmate.
A roomy house provides for their night accomodation. Here
they are kept until ready for sale to the fatteners. Every
care is taken to secure the health of the birds. Cleanliness
in the houses is regarded as a *sine qua non*, and one run is
always vacant, so that each in turn has a month's rest. The
ground is sandy and well drained, but at the time of my visit
was rather moist, as must always be the case under trees,
though probably less with the fir than any other. For
summer rearing it would appear to be everything that could
be desired, giving that shelter from sunshine necessary for
rapid growth. I am not convinced that it is nearly so good
for rearing at other seasons of the year, though the birds
appeared to be thriving and very healthy. Precautions are
taken to avoid infection. The attendants are compelled to
change their shoes before entering the rearing ground. No
stranger (save in such a case as my own) or strange fowl is
allowed among the birds. And if one looks sickly it is
immediately transferred to the hospital. The runs are carefully swept daily, and the manure removed much more than
pays for the labour involved. All food not consumed is
taken away after every meal. When removed from the
incubator and ready for the first feed, a mixture is supplied
consisting of one-third milk and two-thirds water, followed
an hour later by stale wheaten bread crumbs. Although a
little millet is given during the earlier stages, and whole
wheat later, the chief food consists of thirds flour two parts,
and buckwheat meal one part, made into a paste with fresh
skim milk, but in winter oatmeal is used instead of buck-

wheat meal. No meat is given at any period, which is surprising considering how little natural food is obtainable. All the time the vegetable food is supplied abundantly, the finer kinds of garden stuff during the earlier stages, and cabbages, sprouts, &c. later on. It will be seen, therefore, that the food tends to rapid growth and to keeping the flesh soft. As already indicated, nothing but Malines are reared.

57. RESULTS AT LIPPELOO.—Interesting though this enterprise of the Vicomte de Beughem is, the main question will be whether it is financially successful. We have had many similar attempts which were successful in everything except leaving a profit. Upon this point I am able to record the facts. Before doing so, however, it is fair to state that the most careful accounts are kept, showing in detail every item of expenditure and income, even to average production of chickens from eggs sent in by individual farmers. The accounts record that the entire cost, including labour and management, of the chickens at 8 weeks old is 1 franc 23 centimes, or a little less than 1s. each, and at the time of selling when they are 16 to 18 weeks old about 2 francs. They realize 5 to 12 francs the couple, April being the month of top prices. At the time of my visit in November they were selling at 7 francs the couple. The capital invested is 12,500 francs (£600), apart from land and permanent buildings, the latter of which were already in being, and the net profit last year was £200, which is a very satisfactory return. It may, therefore, be regarded as a financial success, especially when we remember that a manager is employed, and that land and buildings not of much use for other purposes are available. If these be valued at an equal amount (£600) to the equipment, the interest is 20 per cent. per annum. The number of birds reared in 1909 was upwards of 10,000.

V.—THE DUCK INDUSTRY.

58. DUCK BREEDING. — Natural conditions in several provinces of Belgium are responsible for the wide distribution of this species of waterfowl, though there are sections not so favourable as are others. Well-watered plains and valleys offer excellent facilities for duck-breeding, and the great rivers with their contributory streams afford favourable opportunities in this direction. In two districts dealt with below, the industry is large and highly specialized. But throughout the country ducks are kept by a great number of farmers, few in number, it is true, but large in the aggregate. There is a very general idea that ducks help to keep the land sweet. Upon what that opinion is based I do not know, but it is undoubtedly true that duck manure is very valuable and fosters the growth of the finer grasses. Evidence of such result has been found in our own land. Around Ghent large numbers of ducks are to be seen, though that is not one of the places referred to. In the Malines market, at the time of my visit, a goodly number were on sale, and in the Campine country this branch of poultry-keeping is extending, though it has not the best land for that purpose. Around Liége, in the valley of the Meuse, many are kept in an ordinary manner. Throughout Flanders and Hainaut ducks are to be found everywhere, and the same can be said as to other districts generally. The demand for these birds is very large, as also for their eggs, which are thought to have the flavour of those of wild birds, and are specially valuable for cooking purposes. The system adopted, with one exception, has been followed for centuries, varying considerably from those met with in England. Belgium has its own breeds, which are referred to in Chapter VIII.

59. HUTTEGEM AND DISTRICT. — One of the most important centres for this industry is in the valley of the Escaut, near the City of Audenarde, in central Flanders, and which I have visited on previous occasions. On both sides

of the river above Audenarde the valley is flat and broad,
flanked by hills of a fair elevation, consisting of water-
meadows, which are flooded in the autumn, remaining under
water until the end of February, when they are drained.
These meadows, which extend several miles from the city
named, beyond the village of Huttegem, are communal
property, and upon these ducklings are raised in large
numbers. Here they find an abundance of rich natural food,
and in return greatly improve the land by their manure. It
is no uncommon sight during March and April to see a
hundred thousand ducklings on the meadows. In April the
birds are removed and the land left for hay. When that
crop is cut the meadows are used for cattle and chickens.
It would be difficult to devise a more complete utilization
of Mother Earth, whose response shows how well balanced
is the rotation. Rich is the soil and ample the return.
When flooded the valley is one vast lake, nearly two miles
in width. The road and dwellings by Bevere, and on to
Huttegem, are just above the water line. It is in these
dwellings where the duck-breeders live. Such is the scene
of a remarkable industry. Cultivation of the fields other
than the water-meadows is good; but the houses are
primitive and not of a high order of comfort.

60. DUCKLINGS AND CHICKENS.—Particulars as to the
breed of duck kept in the Huttegem district are given in
Chapter VIII., which should be studied in view of the
methods adopted, which differs in many respects from those
general in Britain. As a rule each occupier raises 500 to 600
birds annually, but in a few cases the number is greater.
As might be expected, there is considerable difference in the
manner the work is performed. Within the last three or four
years duck-breeding has somewhat declined, though it is still
very extensive, and fowls, chiefly Braekels for production,
have increased greatly in number, as it is found that these
are more profitable and bring a more constant return than
do the ducklings. It is surprising to find that the chickens
are reared on the water-meadows where we might expect
that the conditions would be unfavourable, owing to the wet
ground. That is declared not to be the case. The enormous
amount of natural food obtained on these meadows, more

especially in the shape of worms, &c., is not only valuable and economic in the growth of chickens, but is thought to give feathers the same resistance to water as in the case of ducks. That is an important question for enquiry. The Huttegem breeders state that results in rearing chickens are satisfactory, which is supported by the increasing number of the latter (para. 27.)

61. HATCHING AND REARING.—As a rule, breeding-ducks are accommodated in one of the ordinary farm buildings, which are usually spacious, but cannot be said to conform to our ideas as to light, ventilation or cleanliness. The ducks wander all over the meadows in search of food, but are not allowed out until after they have laid. They return in the evening to their own quarters, when they are shut up for the night. Hens are almost entirely used for hatching, and a local breed called the Huttegem is kept for the purpose. This is a large-bodied fowl, coming into lay very early, and, in fact, becoming broody after producing seven or eight eggs. The maternal instinct is so strong that the hens of this breed will sit for three months without a break, contentedly taking three nests of eggs in succession. They can cover fifteen to seventeen duck eggs, and the plan usually adopted is to transfer the eggs nearly due to such hens as have sat longest, and to increase the number of her brood by additions of ducklings from other hens, as she is only required to protect the young birds against crows, which are the chief enemies, and can look after thirty to forty. Nests are made in warm buildings, and often in bundles of straw. At one place visited forty hens were sitting on eggs. These are fed in an open yard and carefully returned to their own nests as soon as they are satisfied. When the ducklings are hatched they are kept very warm for a couple of days, frequently in the dwelling-room by the side of the fireplace, after which they are transferred to coops made of straw as shown in Plate XII., the photograph for which was taken at Bevere. These coops are placed in the farmyard for a few days, after which they are removed to the open. The reason for the use of straw is that the coop can be easily moved, and when it becomes dirty is burnt to destroy all parasitic life. At first the hens have cords tied to the legs staked in

front of the coops. At a later stage they are put out on the meadows, where natural food is abundant.

62. A SPARTAN SYSTEM.—Hardihood characterizes the Huttegem duck, necessitated by the method followed. Young birds for breeding are employed to secure early eggs, as hatching commences in August, so as to have ducklings ready for January, when sale commences. The season is a short one, ending in April, when the birds are removed from the meadows. It is, as described to me, "a stolen harvest." Rearing upon the Continent of Europe during the winter is more difficult than in the United Kingdom, as the weather is less favourable. Whatever it may be, the ducklings have to bear it; there is no coddling; if too weak they die. On a previous occasion I visited the Audenarde district early in February, when the water-courses were frozen, and the ground covered with snow. Even under those conditions the ducklings were placed out in the open and allowed to go into the water, access to which was given by breaking the ice. The English plan has been to keep the young birds from swimming in water which is very cold, as that is thought to retard growth and induce cramp, but the Flemish peasants do not fear any such consequences. I think it is more than likely this system explains why Huttegem ducks do not attain the same size as our Aylesburys; but that the birds thrive upon it is unquestionable. Huge round hampers with handles, and made bottle-shaped, are used for carrying the ducklings to the meadows and water-courses, and when the flocks are numerous a boy is employed to look after them. The only protection given is by means of hurdles, covered with straw to break the force of the wind. During the earlier stages of growth, the straw coops are usually placed near water-courses, but later the birds wander at will. I was informed that the percentage of loss, except from the depredations of crows, is very small, which speaks well for the vigour of the race. It is recognized, however, that the progeny from eggs laid by very young ducks are weaker than those from older birds, for which reason, as soon as the two- and three-year-old ducks begin to lay, their eggs are preferred for breeding purposes.

63. WATER LENTILS AND WORMS.—As indicated above, the natural food available in these meadows and in the water-courses explains the enormous development of the industry, and why it has proved profitable. The object, therefore, is to make this the foundation, for not only does that mean a great reduction in cost, but the birds are hardier and better able to withstand climatic conditions and variations than if they were fed entirely upon supplied and artificial foods. To this end they are given worms in the infantile stage, and encouraged to seek for them as they grow older. A very strange but common sight in Belgium and some parts of French Flanders is to see the peasants gathering the worms, which are induced to appear on the surface in various ways. Sometimes an iron crowbar is thrust into the ground and well shaken, which causes the worms to come out. But the general method is that the peasants in their *sabots* tread the ground, which has the same effect. The illustration on Plate XIII. shows the latter process in operation. In the rich meadows around Audenarde worms are abundant, as there they find plenty of food and moisture. For the feeding of young birds the peasants pick up the worms and transfer to a bucket or vessel, but when the birds are older they group around the operator and seize the *lumbricus* as they appear; this action on the part of the ducklings is instinctive; they need no instruction or example. Let any-one commence treading the ground, and they will speedily rush to the spot in order to enjoy the feast. There is, how-ever, another article of natural food which is thought to be of almost equal importance, and which is often gathered for the feeding of both chickens and ducklings, namely, what is called *lentille de l'eau* (Latin: *lemna minor*), or the common dock-weed known almost everywhere. It grows largely in the water-courses or ditches, and is eaten with avidity by ducklings. Firm is the belief that this weed is all-important, and that scarcity means a lessened amount of success. The virtue is not alone in the plant, but also the parasitic life found thereon. Hence, when it is gathered for feeding that takes place just before sundown, for the reason that then the water lentils carry a greater number of these parasites than at any other period of the day. Here is a field for enquiry, for it is the first time that I have heard

a suggestion as to the feeding value for poultry of those
minute forms of life which are found upon plants. Such
an investigation might help greatly in the work of raising
all classes of poultry. Moreover, there may be many weeds
now regarded as a curse which might prove a blessing.

64. FEEDING THE DUCKLINGS.—Whilst worms and
plants are chiefly depended upon, these are not enough to
secure rapidity of growth, and food supplied is liberal. For
the first three or four days a mixture of hard-boiled eggs,
chopped fine, buckwheat meal, and Indian meal, and made
into a paste, is fed upon sacks, together with worms, after
which two or three feeds a day are given of either steeped
buckwheat or of buckwheat meal mixed with maize meal,
the birds getting what natural food they can on the
meadows. On this diet they grow well and rapidly, but,
as already stated, do not make the size attained by our
Aylesburys in the same time. There is no fattening in this
section of Flanders. When the ducklings are about six
weeks old they are sold to the duck-feeders at Lebbeke
and Merchtem, referred to later, who finish the work. Early
in the season the price for these young birds is about 12
francs the couple, but later in the season 6 to 8 francs is
the usual rate at which they are sold. At these figures the
profit is substantial. My observations show that duck-
raising is essentially an industry for small occupiers whose
conditions are favourable, and where the standard of life is
modest. Water-meadows are not found with us to the same
extent as in Flanders, but there are many sections of the
United Kingdom, more especially on lower lying lands,
where there is an abundance of moisture, divided by
ditches, that should afford equal opportunities as at
Audenarde. One point to be noted, however, is that the
water-meadows are communal land, and that the flooding
and draining are regulated by local authorities, the peasants
having feeding rights thereon. It is stated that nearly
200,000 ducklings are raised annually in the district, but
that they are decreasing somewhat.

65. LAPLAIGNE.—The other section of Belgium where
duck-raising is carried out on industrial lines is at Laplaigne,

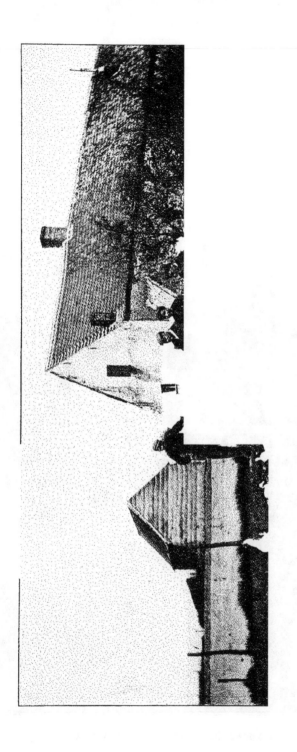

PLATE XIV.—ENCLOSURE FOR YOUNG DUCKS AT LAPLAIGNE ACROSS WATER COURSE.

in the province of Hainaut, on the French border, and like Audenarde on the Escaut River. Here is a great plain, on one side of which is Fontenoy, famous as the scene of an important battle in 1745, when the English and their allies were defeated by the French under Marshal Saxe. It is low lying land, divided by water-courses, and in some cases below the level of the river. A considerable portion consists of water-meadows as at Huttegem, under communal control, and flooded every year. Here is bred a small duck of somewhat uncertain type, but very rapid in growth, producing fine and abundant flesh, which is greatly in demand at Brussels, Lille, &c. I was informed that upwards of 100,000 are produced annually in the commune of Laplaigne, which can be fully credited, for ducklings seem to be everywhere, both in large and small flocks. Three brothers, named Drouillon, are amongst the largest producers, one of whom raises annually about 10,000 birds. One distinctive difference between the Huttegem and Laplaigne ducklings is that the latter are reared practically all the year round. The birds are ready for killing in seven weeks, by which time they weigh 3 to 3½ lb. The flesh is beautifully white and soft. In March and April these birds realize 8 to 10 francs each, but the usual price is 12 to 14 francs the couple.

66. METHODS AT LAPLAIGNE.—In many respects the system adopted resembles that already described in connection with Huttegem, and it is, therefore, not necessary to describe it in detail. But there are differences of importance. In the first place, incubators are here employed almost entirely, made necessary by the fact that the ordinary fowls of the district are Black Braekels, which would be useless as sitters, equally because they are small in size of body and unreliable. The results are said to be very satisfactory, and the introduction of these appliances has led to a great extension of the industry. A second difference is that during the first fortnight the hen and her brood are enclosed during the day within hurdles, which are placed by the side of, and cross, the water-courses, as shown in Plate XIV, where they have access to the small stream, on the banks of which a large amount of natural food is obtained. After that period they are given full liberty. The same system is adopted of helping

them to find worms, as already mentioned, and in the plate named it will be seen that a demonstration was given for our benefit.   Another method I had not seen previously. No artificial heat is provided for the ducklings, but they are very fond of sleeping during the day on beds of fresh stable manure placed in convenient positions, whence they obtain a considerable amount of natural warmth.   Sheds made with hurdles and straw are distributed, into which the ducklings can go when disposed to obtain shelter, and the older ducklings are permitted to wander among the trees, which are found in clumps here and there.

67.   FEEDING AND FATTENING.—As distinct from what has already been stated as to Audenarde, the work is completed at Laplaigne by fattening and killing the ducklings. The method of feeding generally followed is that the food supplied consists of crushed wheat or buckwheat meal, and mixed with cooked potatoes, to which a little meat meal is added.   This mixture is prepared with water into a paste. Probably the reason why meat meal is added arises from the acknowledged fact that, as a consequence of the large number of ducklings bred and kept on the meadows practically all the year round, worms are becoming scarce, as might be expected, for the land does not appear to me to be so rich as at Huttegem.   What effect a continued deficiency of worms will have, and how far it will increase the cost of production, remains to be seen.   That meat will form a good substitute cannot be doubted.   The food named above is continued all the time, but during the last two weeks, when the birds are being fed off, steeped buckwheat forms part of the diet, as that is found to give firmness to the flesh.   When this stage is reached the ducklings are kept in open-fronted sheds with outer yards, so that they do not obtain much exercise, and as a consequence increase rapidly in weight.   At the time of my visit M. Drouillon was building a new brick shed for the accommodation of the birds undergoing the process of fattening.   From all the evidences apparent he and other duck-raisers are prosperous.   At that time he had four men as helpers in addition to his wife and daughter.

68.   LEBBEKE AND MERCHTEM.—As already mentioned (para. 64), one of the great duck-fattening districts is in East

Flanders, around Lebbeke, Opwyck and Merchtem, whence birds are fattened over a wide area for the final process. It is difficult to understand why this part of the work should be specialized, and out of the district where rearing takes place. But such is the case. Here are several men who handle large quantities every year, one of whom has accommodation for 6,000 birds at the same time. On my first visit some years ago objection was raised to allowing an inspection of the birds. At first I thought that it arose from the natural suspicion of Flemish peasants, but that was not the case. The reason was that ducklings are excited by the presence of strangers, and as a consequence make no growth that day, which entails a heavy loss on the owner. This is true with all classes of animals undergoing the process of fattening, for which absolute quietude is all-important. I have found it in chicken, duck, and geese feeding, both at home and abroad. At most of the duck-yards visited special buildings have been erected, consisting of open-fronted brick sheds, generally surrounding an open yard. As a rule the food given consists of buckwheat in water, or buckwheat meal, and whilst the results are satisfactory, I could not but feel that this part of the work is capable of considerable improvement, in that it is upon a less scientific basis than is the case either at Laplaigne or in connection with table poultry at Londerzeel, not to speak of the methods adopted at the great duck centres of England and America, where the maximum of weight at the minimum of cost is obtained.

VI.—GEESE AND TURKEY BREEDING.

69. DECLINE OF THE GOOSE.—As population increases, as land is enclosed and brought under cultivation, geese decline in numbers. That has been evident for a long period of time in the United Kingdom, and statistics with respect to France, Denmark, Italy and America reveal the same influence at work. In no country is that the case more than Belgium, where very few geese are seen, save in two or three districts. For instance, at Renaix I was informed that owing to a large increase of the area of land given up to beet cultivation fields do not now lie fallow, and as a consequence much smaller numbers of geese and turkeys are kept by farmers than was formerly the case. Fowls do no harm to growing crops, but geese and turkeys are heavy birds and require open pasturage. There are three districts where geese are bred in moderate numbers, each of which is on the borders of adjoining countries. The most important of these is at Virtou, in the south-eastern corner of Belgium, close to the French and Luxembourg frontiers, where upon the open lands considerable numbers are reared. A boy, carrying a horn for calling the birds together, is sent out in charge of each flock, and brings them home at night. These geese are chiefly sold in France. On the Dutch border at Vise is a similar, though smaller, industry, but the sale is local. The Liége people go to the village named to feast upon these geese, which are boiled and served with white sauce, forming a special dish not obtainable elsewhere. At Wiers, a village in the Tournai district, a few miles from Laplaigne and close to the French frontier, winter geese are raised in fair numbers. The methods adopted do not call for special notice.

70. FEW TURKEYS. — Equally true is it that turkey-breeding is a very minor part of Belgian poultry breeding, and that comparatively few of these birds are consumed in the country, even at the Christmas period. A partial explanation may arise from the small size of farms in the more highly-cultivated provinces. Reference to paragraph 8 will

show that at the last census only 1·98 per cent. of the holdings were fifty acres and upwards in area. Under these conditions the opportunities for turkey-rearing are strictly limited,
as that species requires plenty of space, and is essentially one
for larger farms. Further, intensive cultivation of the land,
and the small size of the plots given up to each crop, makes
undesirable the presence of large-bodied birds demanding full
liberty to wander anywhere and everywhere. That many
sections of the country might produce much larger numbers
is evident, as indicated by what is stated below respecting
the Ronquières district. The first thing, however, is to create
a demand which at present does not exist, and at paying
prices. The sale of turkeys is chiefly in the summer as prizes
at the archery contests so general at that season of the year.
In nearly every Belgian village may be seen a tall pole on
which are fixed cross-rods intended to afford indulgence in
this sport. Five to six francs in the summer is thought to
be a good price for a turkey designed as a prize, in the
autumn rising to 8 francs, which does not give much encouragement to producers. An attempt, however, is being made
to stimulate the business, as detailed in the succeeding paragraphs. A number of proprietors in other districts keep
turkeys, and I saw an excellent flock of wild birds on the
estate of M. Braconnier, at Modave, in the Ardennes.

71. RONQUIÈRES.—Nearly 20 miles to the south of
Brussels, in the province of Brabant, is the picturesque
village of Ronquières. the centre of a beautiful district,
really a western spur of the Ardenne region. An elevated
tableland, well-wooded and broken up by winding ravines
and valleys, it is a favourite summer holiday resort of the
Bruxellois, who come here for fishing and other sports. In
1569 the Burgomaster of this townlet was beheaded at
Brussels, and also his secretary, who was convicted of
philosophy, for which reason the inhabitants have since been
dubbed " philosophers." They are Walloons, an industrious,
intelligent people, having the reputation of great honesty.
Most of the farms are on high ground, the soil of which
is chiefly loam on slate, though there is some clay. It is
largely arable land, oats and beet being the principal crops,
and cultivation is well carried out. In size the occupations

5

are above the average, ranging from 15 to 60 hectares (37½ to 150 acres). The houses and homesteads are well built, betokening considerable prosperity. Here are favourable conditions for turkey-breeding, both as to nature of the soil, which is dry and warm, and the size of the farms. That, however, is by no means so general as was formerly the case, though there has been an increase of recent years, thanks to the efforts of the burgomaster, M. Michotte, and the schoolmaster, M. de Becker, both of whom I met, and to whose courtesy and help I am indebted. This increase is chiefly among smaller occupiers, for the larger farmers regard the land as too valuable for turkeys. That there would be a great increase is probable if prices were better. The larger farmers only keep poultry for meeting the needs of their own households, and not for sale.

72. TURKEY BREEDING.—That this district has been renowned in some measure for a considerable period is evident. M. de Becker has traced references to turkeys as far back as 1780, but thinks much had been done prior to that time. He says that before then farm contracts for centuries stated that fowls, ducks and geese were to be paid as tribute, but he has found no mention of the turkey in this way. At one period it was customary for nearly all the farmers to keep a breeding pen of turkeys, and rents were paid by the sale of the young stock, which during the month of October were driven to the cities and towns for disposal. With greater cultivation of the land, especially since the introduction of sugar-beet growing, there was a steady decline, so much so that it had almost become extinct. Other contributory causes can be given. Twenty years ago the birds were fed on the stubbles, but now as soon as the corn is harvested the land is ploughed and re-planted, as seen during my drive round the district. As turkeys are not permitted in the woods or on sown fields, their presence is undesirable. The cost of labour has also increased, and children, who at the time named were used as turkey-herds, now go to school. The results were as stated above. Both the breed taking its name from the district and the industry were threatened with extinction. About five years ago the burgomaster, M. de Becker, and others formed a society

with the object of stimulating production in agriculture and horticulture, inclusive of turkeys, as nearly all the old breeders had gone and the younger folk were not taking up the business. The result has been very satisfactory. Although the total stock of turkeys raised in this district is small as compared with the opportunities, every year more farmers are keeping a pen of six to ten birds, and breeding about 100 youngsters each season. Other efforts are being put forth, as shown below, to popularize the turkey, and if a demand can be created at better prices there is no reason why the industry should not grow rapidly, as the conditions are in every way favourable. The observations made, however, show that the people have much to learn with respect to breeding and rearing, as their methods are crude in the extreme, and inferior to those to be found in Great Britain, France and America. In fact, I could come to no other conclusion than, ancient though the pursuit is, the people do not understand the business, and that it is the least progressive and satisfactory branch of poultry-keeping in Belgium. With longer and wider experience, and the dissemination of information as to what is done elsewhere, there is no reason why the near future should not see a marked improvement. At the present time it is estimated there are about 600 to 700 stock turkeys in the Ronquières area, with an annual production of 5,000 to 6,000 young birds.

73. METHODS OF MANAGEMENT.—As a rule stock turkeys are kept with the ordinary fowls around the homestead, all running and sleeping together, and the houses are by no means satisfactory. Under these conditions the best results cannot be looked for. At many of the farms visited the birds appeared very small. It is true that the Ronquières breed of turkey is not so large in size as the American, English or French, but, when fully grown, males will reach 25 lb. The majority of those I saw were not much more than half that weight. The reason for this is that breeders have failed to realize the importance of selecting the best for their own use. Buyers naturally want the biggest specimens they can get, and as these bring a rather better price the people foolishly sell them, retaining for reproductive purposes the smaller and least mature birds, which are generally later

hatched. As these are used as breeding stock in their first year, the tendency is towards enfeeblement of constitution and reduction of size. The Belgians are not alone in making this cardinal blunder, but I do not remember to have seen it carried to the same extent. As a rule, however, the males are chosen more carefully than the hens, which are frequently very small and of all colours. Hatching and rearing are on the usual lines, but M. de Becker has used an incubator for hatching turkeys, in which he obtained an average of 70 per cent., but the chicks were wisely reared by hens. The system of feeding is interesting. For the first two days hard-boiled eggs, chopped fine and mixed with breadcrumbs, are given, after that a paste called *matton*, made of skim milk, bran and hard-boiled eggs, is the staple diet, except that when the birds are about a fortnight old, chopped young nettles are mixed with it, as it is thought that weed is very beneficial, which is doubtless correct. As soon as the change known as " shooting the red " takes place the birds are placed out on the fields and allowed to forage for themselves. If it is found that on returning at night the crops are not filled, then a feed is given of oats and buckwheat..

74. DISPOSAL OF RONQUIERES TURKEYS.—The great majority of the turkeys bred are sold during the summer as *dindon des grains*, that is, when four months old, for the purpose named above, as prizes at archery matches. At that age they weigh 5 to 6 lb., and are similar to the squab turkeys mentioned in my " Report on the Poultry Industry in America " (p. 100). These are taken direct from the fields, and are not fattened in any way. This is a class of bird we do not know in the United Kingdom. If our farmers would extend greatly their production of turkeys, breeding a larger number than they can carry to the Christmas season, a market could be created for part of their flock when three to four months old ; and, further, it will be worth an experiment to see whether small holders could not grow a few turkeys each year, selling them at the age named. I am firmly convinced that consumers only need introduction to these delicate and fine-flavoured birds to cause a very large demand, provided they can be got ready in June and July. So far as the autumn trade is concerned, formerly large

numbers of turkeys were sold to people in the Waterloo district, who fattened them on buckwheat meal, but, with the decline in breeding, that outlet is no longer available. A number are disposed of to be fattened on walnuts and beech nuts. The majority are simply sold in ordinary condition. One of the most important developments, if a demand is to be created for, and a satisfactory trade done in Ronquières turkeys, is that the birds shall be properly fattened. I cannot but think that by such method consumption in Belgium itself would greatly advance, and that a large export trade would grow up, realizing much higher prices for produce than at present. To attain so desirable an object the adoption of more scientific methods is essential, as the present system fails in the directions named above. When it is remembered that the small Laplaigne ducklings, weighing 3 to 3½ lb., sell for 12 to 14 francs the couple, and Ronquières turkeys in October, weighing 10 to 12½ lb., only realize 7½ to 8 francs each, the want of a better system is evident.

75. A TURKEY FAIR.—The formation of a society at Ronquières has been referred to. To its enterprise is due the establishment of an annual fair in the month of September, of which three have been held. The worthy object of these gatherings is to popularize the turkey in Belgium by inducing the great restaurants of Brussels and other cities to make that fowl a leading dish from October 1, onwards, and to advertise the breed. Prizes are offered for the best birds displayed for sale, which can hardly fail to stimulate production on the one hand, as well as help in the creation of a demand on the other. A more practical step could hardly be devised, provided that breeders can be taught improved methods of breeding and rearing, and how to complete their work by the finishing process. The turkey raised in this district is very fine in flavour, but has not hitherto had justice done to it.

76. TURKEYS AND MATRIMONY.—A very interesting gathering was held on the last Sunday of May (Pentecost), 1909, which for its connection with turkeys deserves notice. There was held a *Gouter Matrimonial*, or Matrimonial Feast,

offered by " La Société les Célibataires Repentants," to marriageable girls of the ancient and new world, as stated in the announcements.   These repentant bachelors in search of wives organized a fête with various attractions, including a popular ball, one of which was a feast of turkey sandwiches.   Great crowds attended, inclusive of 3,000 to 4,000 girls, evidently on the outlook for husbands, and some 20,000 sandwiches were consumed.   What have been the results matrimonially I do not know, but that the novel function would help to popularize the turkey is undoubted.   Whether in the main direction of this feast the bachelors referred to regard it as successful I do not know, but that it was of benefit to Ronquières and the district financially, and a stimulus to a greater production of turkeys, is thought to be unquestionable.   It is a novel idea, possible only under simple and primitive conditions.

VII.—MARKETING THE PRODUCE.

77. NEARNESS OF MARKETS. — In considering the methods adopted for sale of the produce in Belgium, the facts already stated as to the density of population and the vast developments of industrial and commercial pursuits must be kept in view, together with the small area of this progressive and enterprising kingdom. Taking the capital city of Brussels as the centre, the following are the distances to the respective frontiers :—

Brussels to Ostend	...	...	78 miles.
,,	Blandain (French)	... ...	57 ,,
,,	Sterpenich (Luxembourg)	...	125 ,,
,,	Dolhain (German)	... ...	83 ,,
,,	Esschen (Dutch)	... ...	50 ,,

Thus the extreme limit is only 200 miles, and, practically speaking, the supplies for all consuming centres are drawn within an area of 30 miles, in the majority of cases much less. The great egg markets of Sottegem and Audenarde are only 28 and 40 miles respectively from Brussels, and Londerzeel, which is the chief table-poultry market, is about 15 miles. From the last-named district the poultry are sent by road to Brussels. Both eggs and fowls are forwarded to Lille and other French towns in the same manner as from Audenarde and Renaix. This nearness to market is a very important factor, as it greatly simplifies the work. A further influence is that the proximity of producers and consumers, together with an abundance of outlets, has prevented the formation of rings or trusts, protecting farmers and others, who, if not satisfied with the prices obtained, are able to secure other markets. As an instance in proof, I was told at Renaix that the demand at Lille determines the price over the whole of Western Flanders, as in fact it does all over the country. Buyers from that city and Brussels compete against each other. When that is so, producers obtain adequate returns. Over the greater part of Belgium similar conditions prevail to what are met with in several districts in Britain where population is concentrated, with the one great difference, namely, that the last-named districts do not provide for their own needs in eggs and poultry, which desirable result has been accomplished in that country. It is estimated that the great county of Lancashire consumes annually eggs and poultry to the value of £2,440,000, and does not produce more than £406,000. Yet it has a vast area of agricultural land, so that production could be enormously developed.

78. NO CO-OPERATION.—In my " Report on the Poultry Industry in Denmark and Sweden " evidence was given that the success achieved, more especially in the former country, has been due to co-operative methods of marketing, not alone in .so far as the great egg societies are concerned, but also that they have advanced the standard of quality, compelling private traders to adopt similar methods in collecting and marketing. But it must be remembered in this connection that Denmark must export, as she has only a small home trade. The same is true in respect to Ireland and Northern Scotland ; but in Belgium it is not so. The first object is to meet the needs of her own people. Denmark has only one large city, Copenhagen, with no other densely-populated areas. In Belgium there are cities such as Brussels, Antwerp, Liége, and great manufacturing and mining districts demanding food supplies. Hence there is no comparison to be made between the two countries except in respect to area of land. What was a prime necessity in Denmark—namely, the finding of a good and regular outlet for produce, with adoption of a system by which the producers could obtain satisfactory returns— does not obtain in Belgium, for there the markets are near by, as close as is Hertfordshire to London, or the Fylde district of Lancashire to Blackburn. Our experience has been that in the immediate vicinity of great centres of population co-operation for sale of food products is not required as in the more remote rural districts, and does not largely enhance prices already obtained, though much can be done to improve methods of marketing. That in some of these districts such improvement could be adopted with advantage in order to secure more rapid passage from

PLATE XV.—Ronquières Turkeys.

farmer to householder is undoubtedly the case, which is also true to some extent in Belgium. As a result of the nearness of markets, so far as I was able to learn there has not been any disposition to form co-operative societies among producers for the sale of eggs and poultry. A number of creameries have been established, but in not a few cases special difficulties have arisen. Possibly as time goes on more may be attempted in this way, and command that loyalty without which co-operation cannot be successful. Belgians are intensely individualistic in many directions. Political and religious divisions have also had some influence in preventing the formation of what are called "syndicates." Upon that question it is unnecessary and undesirable for me to dwell.

79. EGG MARKETS.—In addition to visiting several of of the leading markets, I had the privilege of a long interview with M. Desir de Mulder, of Brussels, President of the Butter and Egg Dealers' Federation, and one of the leading merchants for these products, who gave me a large amount of information. The four great egg markets of Belgium are Nederbraekel, Grammont, Audenarde, and Sottegem, with many smaller, such as Renaix, Malines, &c. As showing the extent of production, M. de Mulder informed me that he had purchased 27,000 eggs in fifty minutes, and 55,000 on one day in April, at Sottegem. The eggs are brought in by farmers once a week, in which respect the system is less satisfactory than that adopted in Denmark and at depôts of the National Poultry Organization Society in England. So long as supplies are consumed locally, or within a few miles, such a plan may answer the purpose, especially where there is practically no competition. If Belgian eggs had to be exported, and to meet those collected at shorter intervals, there is little doubt a modification of this system would be necessary. My observations have shown that the goods are carefully marketed, and a dirty egg is scarcely ever seen. In a previous paragraph (32) mention is made of the care taken to secure clean-shelled eggs, and I notice that nesting material was evidently renewed at frequent intervals, with the same object in view. The eggs are not graded by producers, except that during the autumn and winter months

they are divided into pullets' and hens' eggs. If mixed, the
peasants receive a lower price for them. Sale is by number
and not by weight. In Chapter III (par. 39) particulars as
to ruling prices are given, from which it will be seen that
these are very good indeed, frequently reaching 2d. each
wholesale in winter, which is too dear for exportation to
England. There are plenty of buyers. If those from
Brussels do not offer enough, Lille dealers are at hand, and
vice versa. Any attempt to "ring" the market is easily
defeated. Dealers buy in the open markets, and have packing houses where the eggs are delivered and paid for on the
spot. In many parts of the Campine eggs are still sold by
barter. As the prices of food are extremely high, farmers
make little by the exchange. Eggs are collected every Tues-
day by buyers who go from village to village, a system which
favours the dealer. In summer small-sized eggs often fall
as low as 5 centimes ($\frac{1}{2}$d.) each.

80. PACKING THE EGGS.—Immediately they are received
the eggs are packed in large hampers holding 1,000 each, as
shown in Plate XVI, in which are ten layers, with clean
straw and a sheet of paper between each. On top is a thick
pad of straw covered with canvas, which is then stitched
down. It forms a safe package, easily handled, and of course
the hampers are returnable. So far as I was able to learn,
there is no testing whatever, which speaks well for the producers. Complaints as to quality are sometimes made, and
anyone who attempts to palm off stale or bad eggs is
ultimately found out and soon learns that trickery does not
pay. The packers are very skilful, and speedily discover
any that are doubtful in freshness. In Flanders the great
bulk of the eggs are white in shell, but there and elsewhere
it is customary to pay a slightly higher price for those which
are tinted, as already stated. Duck eggs are exported to
England, where they make a better price than in Belgium.

81. PRESERVATION OF EGGS.—Great though the production of the country, and I was very much impressed with
this in October and November when supplies are usually
very short, the demand in winter is greater than the supply.
To meet the requirements at that season, and to secure the

higher prices of best quality supplies, eggs are imported from Hungary and other countries for cooking purposes. These are preserved, the yolks of which are not firm enough for the best trade. In the egg districts very little preservation takes place, and that chiefly to supply household needs. Some of the Brussels dealers have done a considerable amount of preservation, but have not found it profitable within recent years, due to the rise of prices during April, which is the time of putting down. In fact, at that season there has been very little surplus during the last few years, and at 8 centimes per egg, or nearly one franc per dozen, "the game is not worth the candle." Preserved eggs, in face of Hungarian imports, cannot be sold for more than a penny, even in winter, and when the expenses are taken into account the balance is on the wrong side of the ledger. Moreover, quality can never be so good when the eggs are preserved by dealers in the great cities, as they only put down their unsold stocks, which are not nearly so fresh as if they had been handled at the point of production. As far as can be foreseen it is improbable that this method will increase to any extent, by reason of the fact that a surplusage is not likely to be found. I was informed that mixing eggs is by no means unknown, but it is not practised to any great extent. Trickery is to be met with. A Brussels shop in November exhibited the legend "Eggs, guaranteed fresh, 10 centimes," at a time when new-laids were selling in local markets at 18 centimes each. Everyone knows what that betokens.

82. NOTES OF EGGS.—The following items were supplied to me by M. de Mulder, as the result of his long and wide experience in the egg trade :—

(*a*) Firm yolks in eggs are of essential importance.

(*b*) When hens are fed on maize, yolks are not firm. Further, maize makes yellow or dark yellow yolks, whereas red are desired.

(*c*) Rye produces good quality albumen in an egg. Hens will not, however, eat whole rye. The peasants in the Pays d'Alost make bread with rye meal, short oats and skim milk for their hens.

(*d*) When an egg is round, the yolk is one-fourth greater to the total bulk than if long.

(*e*) When eggs are boiled hard and shells removed the white of brown eggs has a bluish tint, and, also, if cut in two these have more smell than those with white shells. M. de Mulder, therefore, gives support to the theory that brown-shelled eggs are better than whites. Odour is evidently not discernible by chemical analysis.

83. POULTRY MARKET AT AUDENARDE.—Generally speaking, the system followed in the market towns is exactly the same as it has been for centuries. Here producers and buyers meet—the one to sell, the other to purchase. M. Vander Snickt says the scene on market day is exactly the same as he remembers forty years ago, save that the people are better dressed, and there is more produce offered for sale. It is the same week by week, year in, year out. Audenarde only wakens up once a week. During the night before market day the whole aspect of the Grande Place is changed. By 7 o'clock the square is filled with booths for sale of all kinds of merchandise. The side streets are crowded with carts and wagons of every make and shape, from small two-wheeled single vehicles to great hooded wagons, in which the various kinds of produce are conveyed to the French towns. Here are lumbering diligences, under which are crates suspended filled with pigs or fowls. There are dealers' carts loaded up with fowls. The peasants bring a variety of goods in their vehicles. It is estimated that at least 1,500 people visit Audenarde every market day, coming from many miles around. At one season of the year there are more eggs than chickens, at another the reverse. Ducks are not seen here, as they are sent direct to the fatteners. Soon after 7 a.m. the vendors begin to line up in a double row on the east side of the Grande Place with wide avenue between. These are mainly women, with from three to a dozen chickens in a basket. No sale is allowed until 7.45, but on the stroke of the Hotel de Ville clock the buyers rush in, and it becomes a seething mass of humanity. Within fifteen minutes sales are completed, the dealers are packing and loading the produce, and by 10 o'clock all is over. Much of the money received is expended at the booths, and by noon Audenarde resumes its normal aspect, for wagons and people have departed. The birds sold here

are chiefly Brækels, with a few Malines and Huttegems. In the spring enormous quantities of eggs are brought in, but at the time of my visit the number was comparatively small.

84. MALINES MARKET. — Another great centre for poultry is Malines, which lies between the rearing districts of the Campine and the fattening country. It is at this point where the fatteners buy, coming from Londerzeel, Merchtem, and other centres for the purpose. The reason why the finishing does not take place where the birds are reared is that already referred to in Chapter IV.—namely, fattening can only be successful where buttermilk is obtainable, and the Campine is not suitable for cows owing to lack of pasturage. At Malines great quantities of fowls are brought in by the peasants themselves or by higglers who buy from them. Some of the people who do not possess a cart arrive by waggons, paying 25 centimes per bird for carriage, which includes their own conveyance. The majority of the fowls offered for sale were Malines, what is known as the turkey-headed forming a fair proportion, but there were other breeds, and also a fair display of Merchtem ducks, which branch is said to be increasing. The quality of the birds was, on the whole, very good. I was unable to attend the Londerzeel and Merchtem markets, which are very large. At these it is no uncommon thing for 10,000 fowls to be sold on one day, and at Merchtem the returns show that nearly half a million are offered for sale every year. At both these places, however, the area of supply is the immediate district, to which reference has already been made in Chapter IV. Attempts made to introduce private purchase have hitherto failed. The peasants say, with much to justify this opinion, that there is less danger of cutting prices in an open market than if the buyers come round to the farms, for competition comes into play and they have an alternative outlet. In the absence of combination that is undoubtedly correct to a very large extent.

85. BRUSSELS MARKETS.—The short distance which divides Brussels from the fattening centres is all to the advantage of those engaged in this business, as they are

able to personally dispose of their birds. At 6 o'clock every morning a wholesale market is opened in the old abattoirs, to which the fatteners travel by road. The dead fowls are packed in hampers holding twelve to fifteen birds, with straw between, which are placed in front of stands. At six exactly a bell rings, when the hampers are opened and the birds set out. Buyers come round and bargains are made in accordance with the demand. Thus producers sell direct to dealers, and can accept or refuse the prices offered without intervention. When in America I was deeply interested in the method adopted for sale of South Shore roasters at Boston, Mass., which is in the hand of men who undertake the work of killing and plucking. As they keep in the closest touch with the market, attending it regularly, they realize the best prices. If for any reason they decline the rates offered, or supplies are greater than the day's demand, the goods are placed in cold storage for a day or more. I am sure that equally on behalf of private producers and co-operative societies the time is fast approaching when they must sell their own supplies, either directly or by accredited agents, and it was of great interest to see the method adopted in Brussels, for that enables the fatteners to obtain the highest returns in accordance with quality and demand. At any rate they know the state of the market at first hand. This market is provided by the municipality of the city. The whole question of markets requires to be considered in our great cities, but more especially in London, where the system is antiquated and totally unsuited to the requirements of modern times. Not only are purchases made for Brussels itself, but buyers come from Lille and Luxembourg, and large numbers are bought for Germany. At times shipments are also forwarded to Switzerland. The quality of the birds displayed on the morning that I visited this market was very fine indeed, large and meaty, very white in flesh and skin, and with soft bones. The reason why the Malines is so great a favourite arises from the fact that whilst the bones are large they can be cut through with a knife in carving, which can only be when soft and spongy. Dorkings have the same quality. There were a few ducks from Merchtem in the market, good in quality, with white flesh and blue bills. The entire market was cleared in an hour, some 4,000 to 5,000 fowls having been disposed of in that time. It is of interest to note the great growth of the trade with Germany, in spite of the tax of 20 centimes per kilo on all dead poultry imported into that country. These go largely to the Rhine provinces and Berlin.

86.—POULTRY AUCTIONS.—Only the best specimens are offered for sale in the market referred to in the preceding paragraph. Such as are not sold by 7 a.m., or are inferior in quality, are taken to the Halles Centrales for sale by auction. This market has been leased to a syndicate, and all classes of produce are sold. The company referred to has made a good deal of money by its speculation, but I was informed it has not worked to the advantage of fatteners, who have, perforce, to take whatever price the birds realize less the usual charges. Buyers attend in large numbers seeking bargains, chiefly those interested in the cheaper classes of trade, many of whom are women. Not much time is devoted to each lot, and the business progresses at a rapid rate. Nor can it be otherwise. Buyers wish to get through as fast as possible, and the auctioneer has such a crowd of lots to sell, in each of which his pecuniary interest is small. That is, however, always so with second- and third-rate stuff. If fatteners gain by the system previously noted, as compared with our own, in this case they are liable to lose. The auction mart is seldom a satisfactory place for the vendor.

VIII.—BELGIAN RACES OF POULTRY.

87. EFFECT OF VARIED CONDITIONS.—In the opening chapter references are made to the diversified conditions met with in Belgium, and to the intensified methods adopted for the production of food supplies. As might be expected, the result of such conditions is evident in the large number of breeds of poultry to be found within the Netherlands. Those who are interested in British live stock do not need more than the fact to be stated. One supreme reason for the large number of breeds of horses, cattle and sheep to be found in Britain is that here we have variations of soil, of elevation, of aspect, and of climate, to an extent not met with in any other country. Breeders have endeavoured to evolve and maintain races of the animals named suited to their special environment. That they have succeeded is apparent to everyone. To some extent the same result has been attained with poultry, but to a lesser degree. Farmers, as a rule, have not concerned themselves with this class of stock, and have left improvement largely in the hands of fanciers and exhibitors, who do not care whether the locality suits the fowl or the fowl the locality. In fact, limitation of area, over which a breed should be kept for practical purposes would be antagonistic to the interests of this class of breeders, whose object naturally was, and is, to find customers everywhere. To some extent, however, Nature has shown that certain breeds yield better results in given districts than do others, and as poultry receive more attention from farmers, large and small, the tendency will be for a greater uniformity to be attained over areas where the conditions are fairly equal. I do not suggest that we should not test new breeds with a view to seeing if they will give greater returns than those we already possess, for that would be foolish in the extreme. Had such a policy been adopted in the past the progression seen within recent years would not have been made. There are, however, manifest advantages for practical poultry breeding if the birds found within a given district

are uniform, securing a distinctiveness to the production of that district which is an important asset. Everyone will acknowledge that the success achieved by the duckers of Buckinghamshire owes much to the Aylesbury duck. Had the breeders kept all classes of ducks the story would have been very different from what has been the case. In Belgium, as also in France to a lesser extent, variation of breed is as great as is the variation of conditions. It has been an object, probably for centuries, that each district should maintain the breed or breeds best suited to it, and, practically speaking, no other, for there they yield the best results. Some breeds improve by change from one place to another, but not those which have been brought to a high state of perfection and productiveness, as they frequently deteriorate in both respects when removed from the home of their race. In this respect there is no universal law. I have found that the Braekel did not thrive as well in England as it does in Flanders, and that the Bresse proved a better layer in Britain than in south-eastern France, but not so good on the table. That, however, is a question which does not concern us now. Suffice it to say that in Belgium each district has its own breed, whether native or imported.

88. INTRODUCTION OF NEW BREEDS.—Whilst what has just been stated is true, it must not be thought that the Belgians have refused to keep any breed except it were indigenous to the country, for that is not so. We have already seen (par. 35) how great an influence the Italian or Leghorn has had, and also that the Orpington has been received with favour. Undoubtedly fanciers and exhibitors have had much to do with the introduction of these and other breeds. I was assured that the class of breeders just named have done a great amount of harm by the introduction of new breeds, and by tempting Belgian peasants to sell their best birds, leaving poor stock behind. That opinion may be correct, and probably is fully justified, specially the latter and where breeds are made popular regardless of their economic qualities. But experience has shown that if the right breed is selected, change of conditions and of environment stimulates productiveness. M. Louis Vander Snickt, states that he believes removal of any fowl

6

from a warmer to a colder climate compels activity of body and reduces the fatty reserves, so that the hens lay better than they do under the original conditions. He attributes to this the great prolificacy of Leghorns in Belgium, Denmark, Britain, and America. On the other hand, removal from cool to warm climate increases the fat and flesh, induces lethargy, and reduces the number of eggs produced. If that theory is correct, much will be explained hitherto unknown. Belgians possess a great knowledge as to the science of breeding, but refuse to reveal it. They are said to have known and practised Mendel's law for centuries.

89. DISTRIBUTION OF BREEDS.—Although many new breeds have been introduced into Belgium by amateurs and exhibitors, the greater part of these have exerted no influence whatever upon the general class of poultry kept in the rural districts, as they are chiefly found in the suburban and manufacturing districts. That, however, is not absolutely true. I have already mentioned the Leghorn and the Orpington, especially the former, as having profoundly influenced the poultry industry of Belgium. Another instance is the Minorca, which, introduced about a dozen years ago, has spread over a considerable part of the provinces of Liége and Brabant. Speaking generally, the areas over which the different breeds are distributed are as follows : The Braekel fowl is chiefly kept in the Pays d'Alost, which includes East Flanders, a part of West Flanders, and a portion of Hainaut ; the Campine fowl is found on the sandy plains of the provinces of Antwerp and Limburg ; Malines fowls are mainly bred within a radius of 20 miles around the City of Malines, Brussels and Antwerp, Termonde and Aerschot forming the border lines, with a tendency to extend further east and west as demand increases ; the five-toed Courtrai fowl, undoubtedly owning the same ancestry as our Dorking, is found in West Flanders on the French border ; the Huttegem fowl is limited to a small area around the City of Audenarde ; game fowls are met with in all parts of the country, but especially in Western Flanders, in which province large numbers of farmers run these birds for cock-fighters ; the Brabant fowl is met with in the province of that name to the south of Brussels ; the Minorca fowl has found

great favour in Southern Brabant, Eastern Hainaut, and part of Liége ; over the greater part of Namur and Belgian Luxembourg the Ardennes fowl is distributed ; the Herve fowl has its home on the tableland of Eastern Liége, between the City of Liége, Verviers, and the German border near Aix-la-Chapelle; in the southern corner of Belgium is a crested breed of fowls ; and Leghorn fowls are distributed over a wide area outside Flanders. The Merchtem duck is to be seen a little to the north of Brussels; the Blue Termonde duck, to a lesser extent, on the low-lying meadows around Termonde in East Flanders ; the Huttegem duck near Audenarde ; and the Laplaigne duck on the higher reaches of the Escaut river, adjacent to the French border. Geese are met with at Wiers, Vese and Virtou respectively, and turkeys in the Ronquières district, as already stated. There are many other breeds of poultry kept in the country, but those named above are best known.

90. QUALITIES OF RACES.—It is not necessary for the present purpose to attempt a description of the various Belgian breeds of poultry. Those who desire to study the subject more fully will find a chapter devoted to these in my work on " Races of Domestic Poultry."[1] But it is desirable that something should be said in a few instances as to the qualities by which the breeds have attained pre-eminence, and in some cases held a prominent place in the egg and poultry production of Belgium for a very long period. Two points in this connection should be emphasized : First, that whilst the external characteristics of the respective breeds have been kept in view, evolved probably as a result of natural conditions, productiveness has been the determining factor ; and, second, the fact has been recognized that to secure prolificacy in respect to egg production a small-sized body is essential. Hence we find all the laying breeds are small, and the table breeds large. A big frame means inactivity and lethargy, so that the eggs are fewer than where an active habit, combined with small body, is met with. The Belgians have recognized this fact,

---

[1] London : Edward Arnold, 1906.

for fact it is. I was glad to find the view held very firmly that in-breeding causes degeneracy in size of egg and reduction of number, as well as lessened vigour of constitution, which may be commended to those who are practising and recommending what I cannot but regard as false methods of breeding. A new point to me is that the colour of earlobe is regarded as important, in that a red earlobe is said to accompany meat properties, a white earlobe egg production, and that a smooth earlobe betokens smooth shell of egg. Upon these theories careful observations should be made.

91. BRAEKEL AND CAMPINE FOWLS.—These two races own the same ancestry, and are similar in all respects save size of body, which is rather larger in the Braekel, as a result of being kept on the rich land of Flanders. They are prolific layers of large eggs. It is suggested that originally both breeds were related to the Bresse fowl of France. For a long period Belgium and Burgundy were under one Crown, during which time intercommunication would be constant. Braekels are great foragers, and do not thrive where the soil is thin. When kept near woods they forage all day, only returning home in the evening. As a rule they are non-sitters, but enough become broody to meet ordinary farm requirements. Recognizing the importance of keeping the bodies small, cocks are mated early, and precocity in egg production of pullets has the same effect. As a rule May and June are the best months for hatching Braekels, and also Campines. If brought out early the pullets will lay about twenty eggs and then become broody, but if hatched at the time named they come into profit in the autumn and go right on without desiring to sit. When about eight weeks old they are small in bone and very fleshy, excellent as *poulets de lait*. After that the table qualities are very moderate. Braekel eggs have a large red yolk with strong membrane, and the albumen or white bears a smaller proportion to the whole than with eggs of other breeds.

92. MALINES FOWL.—Cuckoo-coloured fowls appear to have been bred for centuries in Belgium, but probably resembling the type of the Coucou de Flandre, which is met with to a limited extent on the French border, rather

than the present-day Malines. That is a composite fowl
in which the breed just named, together with Langshan and
Antwerp Brahma, are combined. It is a large, somewhat
slow-growing fowl, with soft, spongy bone which can easily
be cut through, and responds to fattening. The legs are
slightly feathered. It is suggested that such feathers are
associated with a big skeleton and spongy bone, and clean,
ivory-scaled legs with hard bone. At first there was only
one variety, the Cuckoo, but others have been introduced
by crossing, primarily by exhibitors. White Malines are
not much kept except for fancy. A more recent variety is
that known as the turkey-headed Malines, by which is
meant that the birds have no comb or wattles. These are
becoming very popular in the Campine country, where they
are said to be quicker in growth than the single-combed
variety. They were produced by crossing the Bruges
Game on the ordinary Malines. They are moderate layers,
but make big birds, and the chickens are said to grow at
the rate of 2 lb. per month, and when matured weigh from
10 lb. to 14 lb. The fatteners, however, do not regard
them as equal to the ordinary Coucou de Malines in meat
qualities, as the flesh and bone are harder.

93. BRABANT FOWL.—Upon the higher lands of
Brabant where the soil is thin over stone or slate, the
Braekel does not thrive, as the conditions are too severe.
A hardy, vigorous breed is essential, which explains the
popularity of the Leghorn. The same is true on the hills
of West Yorkshire and East Lancashire, as in other parts
of Britain. The native race, called by the name of the
province, meets these requirements. It is stated to be a
very old race, and has considerable affinity with the Dutch
Crested Fowl, as it has a good-sized crest. It is much
larger in size of body than the Braekel, a good layer, and
when young carries a large amount of flesh, which, together
with the skin, is white. My observations indicate that it is
not increasing in popular favour, due partly to the introduction of the Leghorn.

94. ARDENNE FOWL.—Throughout the mountainous
districts of South-Eastern Belgium, known as the Ardennes,
thinly populated and sparsely cultivated, poultry are not

much kept. There, however, over a large area is found a breed of medium size bearing this name. As might be expected, essential requirements are vigour of constitution and activity of habit. These the Ardenne Fowl possesses. It has evidently much of the game in its composition, both as to colour and shape of body, and also that it is better in meat properties than as a layer. Under the conditions named it is inexpensive to feed, as it forages widely, and therefore is found profitable, which would not be the case if all the food had to be supplied.

95. HERVE FOWL.—As previously mentioned (para. 35), on the high tableland to the north-east of Liége is a breed not found elsewhere in Belgium. The district is cold and exposed, with a soil rich and productive. The Herve breed is small in size, weighing $2\frac{1}{2}$ to $4\frac{1}{2}$ lb., but excellent as a layer, producing eggs of average size. M. Weerts informed me that he had hens which yielded 130 to 140 eggs per annum on a farm under ordinary conditions. There are three varieties, but I saw more Blacks than any of the others. The Herve is a breed which is capable of great improvement, though its small size would not recommend it. On small occupations that should be no disadvantage. The other Belgian breeds of fowls, save those named below, do not call for special mention.

96. RUMPLESS FOWLS.—In nearly all countries races of fowls are to be met without tails. The cause for this loss of tail has never been explained. In some sections of the Province of Liége these birds are kept because it is thought they are better able to escape from foxes and other enemies, who have much less to seize upon. If that is so, it is another instance of "survival of the fittest," and of natural adaptability to special conditions. So far as I am aware, birds having this peculiarity are looked upon as sports, interesting it is true, but nothing more. The Belgians, however, think that there is a practical value in the absence of tail feathers, and state that such birds grow more rapidly than those fully feathered, making flesh one-third greater in the same period. This is a new idea, one worthy of enquiry. I have always regarded feathers as the most expensive part of the fowl to produce, and for that

reason have depreciated their undue development as in some fancy breeds of poultry. M. Paul Monseu says that it costs five times as much to feed feather as it does flesh. That this body covering is needed by birds for warmth and flight is well known, but as we do not desire our fowls to fly, so much less is required, save that in table breeds a curtailment of the wing flights would certainly result in reduction of the motor muscles on the sternum or breast. The question, however, requires further investigation before a definite opinion can be expressed. When in America I saw a large number of growing chickens in which the feathers were checked in growth, and the opinion was expressed that the bodies of these grew more rapidly. In Britain we often find that artificially-raised chickens do not feather as evenly as those brought up under hens. That is a weakness which needs to be combated, and is very different from the absence of parts of plumage, such as the tail, which are not required. My view of the matter is supported by table poultry-breeders in Belgium, who state that slow-feathering birds are more delicate in constitution than those which grow the plumage naturally. Small-sized fowls assume their feathers more rapidly than these heavier races. Comparisons must, therefore, be made between birds of the same breed. It is interesting to note that M. Robert Pauwels, of Everberg, Brabant, is producing several new rumpless, or tail-less, types of fowls.

97. UTILITY BANTAMS.—The claim has frequently been made by English breeders of Bantams that there is no class of fowl which is so profitable, whether as egg or meat producers, as these diminutive races, taking into account the space occupied by them and the cost of food. For market purposes it would be useless keeping them, owing to the small size of body and of eggs produced, though as to the former it is an open question whether a demand could not be created. In Belgium what has been stated above is widely accepted, and there is probably no country where so many Bantams are kept as there, chiefly by residents in towns and manufacturing centres. This is not merely a question of fancy or exhibition, though these do enter into it, but for the supply of household needs. In the Liége district many

miners breed Bearded Bantams, and often obtain an average of 150 eggs per annum from each hen, all of which are consumed at home. It is for that reason the Bantam and other clubs advocate the encouragement of breeding this type of fowl specially for the sake of the children, who would probably never taste an egg if large fowls were kept, as their parents would be tempted to turn them into money. This is a more important point than at first sight appears, and deserves consideration on the part of all who are interested in development of the poultry industry and encouragement of home production. If the eggs and chickens are consumed in the household that is a great gain. Hundreds of thousands of Bantams might be maintained in our great centres of population. Hitherto we have not looked upon Bantams as utility fowls, but the question is worthy of careful enquiry. My friend, M. Louis Vander Snickt, says there should be three types of every race of fowl ; first, large for table purposes ; second, medium for egg production ; and, third, Bantams for working people with limited space at command. Exhibition Bantams are largely kept, and some of the races are wonderful in the extreme. The establishments of M. Van Gelder, President of the Bearded Bantam (Barbu Nain) Club, at Uccle, near Brussels, and of M. Robert Pauwels, at Everberg, are well arranged, and include wonderful specimens of the breeder's art. M. Van Gelder's Porcelaine and Quail Bantams are among the most beautiful specimens of poultry I have ever seen, especially the former.

98. COCK-CROWING CONTESTS.—At the First National Poultry Conference in 1899 M. Vander Snickt caused considerable astonishment by stating that the crow of the cock has a definite economic value, in that it is indicative of profitable qualities. That was a new idea in this country, yet is generally accepted in Belgium. We would like to check crowing; the Belgians encourage it, largely, however, for sport. Among many classes, especially miners, this is a great pastime, and is said to have a moral influence in that the breeding and training of the birds keep the men at home, whilst the eggs laid and surplus birds help to feed their families. Cock - crowing contests are very popular

among the industrial population in several districts, and the sight is a very interesting one. Some birds will crow 250 times in half an hour. Upon that side I need not dwell. My object is to state what the crow indicates. Every poultry-keeper knows that there is a great difference in the age at which the young cockerels begin to crow, and that the races in which the cockerels crow earliest are those in which pullets lay soonest, by reason of the fact that they grow fastest. A Leghorn cockerel will attempt to crow when half the age of an Orpington, and the age at which pullets of these breeds begin to lay bears about the same relationship. Upon the importance of this function Belgian breeders lay much stress. A cockerel does not crow until his comb has developed and is red, and we know that there is a connection between the comb and the reproductive organs. Precocity in one indicates activity in the other. How far the frequency of crowing or its prolongation may be accepted as proof of any economic quality I should not like to say, but the subject is worthy of investigation. Early crowing in cockerels we know means early laying in pullets bred at the same time from the same parents. It is claimed that frequent crowing tells of a salacious disposition and ability to serve a large number of hens, and that prolonged individual crows betoken prolificacy in the pullets. If these theories are sound the cock - crowing contests have an economic value.

99. BREEDS OF DUCKS.—It is not necessary that the races of domestic waterfowl shall be dealt with at any length. Of ducks the Merchtem and Huttegem are most prominent. The former is white in plumage, with creamy legs and a blue bean on the bill. It is similar in shape to the Aylesbury, but smaller in size of body. The ducks are excellent layers, and the ducklings very rapid in growth, with fine-quality flesh. Huttegem ducks are rather larger, and, as previously mentioned (para. 62), are very hardy indeed. They are upright in carriage, have longish neck and legs. The body is white, with coloured head and neck, and blue beak, legs, and feet. Quick in growth, they are ready for fattening when about six weeks old. Laplaigne ducks are small (para. 65), and somewhat uncertain in colour.

The Blue Termonde duck is much larger in size than any of those named, and for later and more fully-matured specimens is excellent, but these are not kept to any great extent as they do not grow with sufficient rapidity.   There is, however, a distinct predisposition towards blue - plumaged ducks, as they are not so easily seen at night as the whites. Black ducks are thought to be finest in flavour of flesh, whilst blues, which are produced by crossing black on white, have the flavour of blacks and the flesh colour of whites. To improve the quality of flesh a blue drake should be mated with white ducks, but to secure vigour a yellow or cream-feathered drake, such as the Pekin, gives the best results. I am unable to speak personally as to the races of geese.

100.   RONQUIERES TURKEY. — In Chapter VI. some particulars are given as to the breeding of this turkey, the only one which, so far as I know, can be called a native of Belgium.   From the appearance it would seem that it is a composite breed, probably having the French Black as the basis, though from the metallic reflections on the wings it is not improbable that Bronze American blood has been introduced.   There is great divergence in colour of plumage ; in fact, so long as the legs and feet are white, with white toe nails, the feather colour is regarded as of secondary importance.   In the hands of a few skilled breeders the Ronquières turkey could be greatly improved.   Of good size, with beautifully white, soft and fine-flavoured flesh, it ought to occupy a much higher position in Belgium than is the case to-day.

101.   BREEDING THEORIES.—The following items, reproduced from my notes, represent ideas held by breeders in Belgium, as supplied to me by M. Louis Vander Snickt. They are of sufficient importance to warrant consideration. I do not advocate their acceptance without further enquiry.

(a) For improvement of races of poultry in any country birds should be selected which have been brought up in a hardy manner and of small size, as these improve greatly under better conditions.   It is regarded as a mistake to use highly-bred stock for practical purposes, as there is always decadence as a result of ultra refinement.

(b) Black or dark - plumaged fowls should have white under-colour, especially where extremes of temperature are met with. It is thought to be injurious for the surface colour to be carried through to the skin. Black absorbs, and white reflects, heat.

(c) To make birds or animals breed give them the same food as they would have when in the infantile stage.

(d) When a hen is sitting her feathers throw off no smell, so that the scent of her enemies is in vain. It is stated that a fox will not be able to discover a sitting hen if she is out of sight, even though he passes within a yard or two. The elements which ordinarily cause the smell go into the intestines, and are carried off by the manure, which is always most odorous in a sitting hen.

(e) In winter breeding ducks must have access to water or the eggs will be infertile.

(f) Belgian peasants do not like big trees on their farms, as these are thought to exhaust the ground.

IX.—INSTRUCTION IN POULTRY-KEEPING.

102. LECTURES.—Comparatively little has been done hitherto in Belgium for direct teaching in connection with the poultry industry. That may be due to the fact that the peasants in that country are already skilful at this work, and have very little to learn. Or, as expressed to me, they know more of the subject than those who might be sent to teach them. Such may be true in certain directions and over given areas. But it is not the case taking Belgium as a whole. Even in Flanders, where poultry-breeding reaches its highest development, whilst as to breeding the peasants have a knowledge which commands admiration, there is much required in the way of improvement of method. Moreover, one great advantage of instruction is reporting what is being done elsewhere. That Belgian farmers are willing to adopt progressive methods is evident from the increase of artificial methods of hatching and rearing in the Malines and Laplaigne districts, and they should be fit subjects for instruction. A limited number of lectures are given in the rural districts every year, but it is recognized that these are totally inadequate to the importance of the subject. In 1908, 373 such lessons were given, and in 1909 371. In the last-named year courses of from one to four lectures were provided in 123 villages, the arrangements for which are made by the Fédération Nationale des Sociétés d'Aviculture de Belgique, which body annually submits a scheme to the Minister of Agriculture, who, on approval, makes grants for payment of the lecturers, usually certified agriculturists. In 1909 the appropriation for this purpose was only 5,565 francs (£222 8s.), which works out at 15 francs per lecture. No charge is made to students, and those who attend not less than three lectures are permitted to sit for an examination, theoretical and practical. Such as obtain not less than 60 per cent. of total marks, or not less than 50 per cent. of the marks in each subject, are awarded official certificates of capacity, the value of which must depend upon the knowledge of poultry-keeping

possessed by the student previous to taking the course, for three lessons would be useless otherwise. Probably, however, every student possesses a considerable amount of knowledge, in which case the certificate, if the examination be strict, is worth much more than at first sight would appear.

103. AGRICULTURAL COLLEGES.—It is evident that the same spirit is manifest in Belgium in respect to poultry as we have had to contend against in Great Britain, due to an utter want of realization of the importance of this branch of live stock. In the provision of agricultural instruction at rural schools poultry-keeping holds a place, but a very minor one at that, and the same is true at agricultural colleges. The regulations issued by the Minister of Agriculture, whilst providing for this subject in the zoology courses, relegate it to an inferior position. As a consequence it is not surprising that very little is done. At Gembloux, where is a fine State Agricultural College, with splendid buildings and equipment in nearly every branch, there is no poultry plant whatever, and the same is true at Louvain. At Gembloux the director, Mons. C. Hubert, informed me that he has made a requisition for 3,000 francs (£120) in order to commence practical teaching and demonstration of poultry-keeping, but this very modest request was refused, and he was only able to obtain 1,000 francs (£40). In the museum at Gembloux are a few models and pictures, but these do little more than demonstrate their inadequacy. Professor Racquet, head of the Zoological Section, gives lectures on poultry to the students. He, however, is handicapped by want of means for extension and for practical demonstration. It is deeply to be regretted that this splendid institution, with its great opportunities, should not deal with aviculture in a suitable manner, in view of its great importance to the entire country. The influence upon the 160 agricultural students must be serious. They cannot but feel that on the judgment of the authorities poultry is a negligible quantity, and need not be considered. A little has been done in experimental work as stated below, but in that case also small as compared with the need. I found the director and professors keenly alive to the importance of this subject, eager to do it justice, but unable to accomplish their desires.

104. SPECIAL POULTRY SCHOOLS.—I was informed by the Minister of Agriculture that there is not in Belgium any State poultry school. Some lessons are given in aviculture at Londerzeel, where is a horticultural school, and at Gembloux to the extent named above. This lack would not be felt if the two great agricultural colleges, Louvain and Gembloux, were dealing adequately with the subject. At Westmalle, in the Province of Antwerp, is what is called a " Ferme-École Professionnelle Pratique d'Aviculture," conducted by M. Leon Lacroix upon his own responsibility. Here lectures are given in French and Flemish, and the course extends over at least three months. Instruction is both theoretical and practical, and in association with the school is a poultry farm, said to be well equipped, but as I had not an opportunity of visiting it my information is second-hand. The cost of instruction, inclusive of board and lodging, is 350 francs (£14) for three months. This school was established in 1903, and nearly forty students have been trained in it, several of whom are now engaged as poultry-breeders in the neighbourhood of Londerzeel. The farm comprises 150 acres, largely used for agricultural students, the poultry section of which occupies about 2½ acres. Instruction is above all practical, but theoretical courses are given twice a year in accordance with the programme issued by the Minister of Agriculture, but, being a private venture, no subsidy is received. Silver Campines are kept for egg production. More attention is, however, given to the rearing of Malines, as they yield a greater profit. At Thimister, in the Herve country, an attempt was made some time ago to establish what it was hoped would be a teaching centre for that section of Belgium, but it has not proved financially successful, and is now conducted by Mons. L. Weerts as a private breeding farm and demonstration plant. The equipment is good as far as it goes, but is limited in extent. There are no students on the farm, but it renders a great service, in that schoolmasters are permitted to bring their pupils on visits from time to time. To build up any industry it is necessary to get hold of the younger folk, as only one adult in fifty will learn and adopt new methods. M. Weerts lectures for the Federation, and also such communes as desire courses, and practical men

like him can do much if they are afforded an opportunity. But teaching plants cannot be conducted properly on a commercial basis. If the sale of fowls and appliances, as at Westmalle and Thimister, has necessarily to be given a primary position, the students suffer. Moreover, there is always a danger of promoting such sales within limited lines, and that advice is unconsciously influenced by a desire to encourage the business side. Hence, public funds and control are indispensable for the success of educational establishments. A further point is that if fees charged have to suffice for meeting the expenses, that section of the community who need the benefit of instruction most cannot afford the cost. I was informed that in the Herve district there are several dairy schools, that being the great butter country, and it is surprising no attempt has been made to include poultry instruction in their respective courses. The great increase of poultry in the Herve section of Belgium on the dairy farms shows that the two branches work together advantageously.

105. EXPERIMENTAL WORK.—One of the most valuable means of education is in the conduct of practical experiments, and there is no branch of agriculture in which such investigations are needed more than in poultry-keeping. In Europe this work has hitherto received very little attention. As pointed out in my " Report on the Poultry Industry in America," that is not the case in Canada and the United States. More experiments have been conducted in respect to poultry in the State of New York than in the whole of Europe, from the Ural Mountains to the Atlantic Ocean. In this direction Belgium is no better than its neighbours. The Fédération Nationale des Sociétés d'Aviculture de Belgique has expended part of its funds in this direction, and would have done much more had money been available. At Gembloux experiments in the fattening of Merchtem ducks and Malines fowls have been carried out, specially to compare the value for this purpose of buckwheat and barley, and also natural *versus* artificial methods of rearing. M. Weerts has conducted feeding observations at Thimister, and the Liége Poultry Society (L'Union Avicole de Liége) has also subsidized, to a limited extent, experimental work.

At Gembloux I found that in addition to the director, Professor Racquet, already named, Professor M. Schille Gregoire, head of the State Chemical and Bacteriological Institute, and his assistant, M. Carpiaux, are all deeply interested in poultry, and fully realize the great necessity for research. They have the qualifications and the opportunity, but the means are wanting. It is the latter, a denial of which in Europe has prevented greater development of the Poultry Industry. With increased production and greater intensification of method the need for experimental work becomes more urgent, equally to secure enhancement of returns and reduction of cost, and to prevent loss by disease, the risks of which are correspondingly greater as numbers increase upon the same area of ground. In the direction of experimental work Belgium is distinctly lacking.

X.—GENERAL NOTES.

106. INTER-COMMUNICATIONS. — Development of the resources of any country is largely dependent upon the facilities afforded for bringing producers into immediate and direct communication with the consuming centres. It is useless extending the output unless there is a profitable outlet, which can be reached at the minimum of expense. This is essentially a question for producers, who have ultimately to suffer should there be any hindrance to sale of or excessive cost in reaching the markets. Under intensive systems that is even more important than was the case formerly. In this respect Belgium is specially favoured. A small country with a large population, there are no long distances to be traversed ere the point of consumption is reached. Further, alternative markets are at hand, so that prices are well maintained. At one period rivers and canals were the means of traffic between one place and another. Then came the time of roadways. Now railways intersect the country in every direction, not alone the great State trunk lines, but also the " Vicinal " or light railways, which are found almost everywhere, linking up the ordinary railroads. Reference to the map of Belgium will indicate the wonderful development of these light railways, which seem to run in all directions and serve many areas which the main railways do not touch. The result has been a great increase of prosperity in the rural districts. Again and again has evidence been brought forward as to the value of these connections, simple and inexpensive as they are, built without the heavy cost of the ordinary railroads, passing along the roadways where the people are, and connecting villages which were near in mileage but remote in reality. To serve the people has been the first object, but it has paid well to do so. Markets are now available to producers which were too far away before, or involved a roundabout and expensive journey. A further sign of progress is the universal use of the electric light throughout the villages and smaller towns. I could not but compare unfavourably the condition of things in our own country, so far as that is concerned. Some of our villages have not got beyond the oil stage, which in Belgium would have electricity, not because mechanical power is cheaper there or oil or gas more expensive, but from some other reason. In fact, progress and prosperity are evidenced on all sides. The people eat white bread where they once consumed rye.

107. RAILWAY RATES.—Belgium is not alone a land of railways, but it is also one of cheap rates. An ordinary third-class passenger ticket for 100 miles only costs 3 francs 80 cents. (3s. 2d.), which is 5s. 2d. less than it would be in Britain, and a return ticket for the same distance is only 6 francs 05 cent. (5s.). By the courtesy of M. de France, representative of the Belgium State Railways in London, and the Superintendents of the Great Eastern and Great Western Railways Companies, I am able to give comparative figures for the two countries as far as these are possible. One important point must be kept in view—namely, that there are no owner's risk rates in Belgium, all goods being consigned at company's risk. For purposes of comparison I have selected (1) Audenarde to Brussels, 40 miles, and (2) Londerzeel to Liége, 65 miles, and worked out similar distances on the two English railways named.

EGGS AND POULTRY PER PASSENGER TRAIN.

Miles	Company	Company's risk	Owner's risk
40 ...	Belgian State ...	4s. 0d. per 2 cwt. ...	—
,, ...	G.E. Ry. Co. ...	4s. 0d. ,, ...	3s. 8d. per 2 cwt.
,, ...	G.W. Ry. Co. ...	9s. 4d. ,, ...	4s. 8d. ,,
65 ...	Belgian State ...	5s. 7d. ,, ...	—
,, ...	G.E. Ry. Co. ...	5s. 4d. ,, ...	3s. 9d. ,,
,, ..	G.W. Ry. Co. ...	14s. 0d. ,, ...	7s. 0d. ,,

EGGS PER FAST GOODS TRAIN.

Miles	Company	Company's risk	Owner's risk
40 ...	Belgian State ...	12s. 6d. per 10 cwt. ...	—
,, ...	G.E. Ry. Co. ...	12s. 3½d. ,, ...	10s. 7½d. per 10 cwt.
,, ...	G.W. Ry. Co. ...	18s. 11d. ,, ...	12s. 6d. ,,
65 ...	Belgian State ...	18s. 1½d. ., ...	—
,, ...	G.E. Ry. Co. ...	15s. 5d. ,, ...	13s. 1½d. ,,
,, ...	G.W. Ry. Co. ...	24s. 0d. ,, ...	17s. 6d. ,,

POULTRY PER FAST GOODS TRAIN.

Miles	Company	Company's risk	Owner's risk
40 ...	Belgian State ...	12s. 6d. per 10 cwt. ...	—
,, ...	G.E. Ry. Co. ...	10s. 10d. ,, ...	—
,, ...	G.W. Ry. Co. ...	18s. 4d. ,, ...	
65 ...	Belgian State ...	18s. 1½d. ,, ...	
,, ...	G.E. Ry. Co. ...	12s. 11d. ,, ...	
,, ...	G.W. Ry. Co. ...	24s. 2d. ,, ...	

The transit charges for ordinary goods train in Belgium for eggs and poultry is 6s. 11d. per ton for 40 miles and 10s. per ton for 65 miles. It will be seen, therefore, that rates are lower in certain directions in Belgium, but not in others, and that in some cases our producers have the advantage.

108. NATIONAL FEDERATION OF POULTRY SOCIETIES.— A large number of poultry societies exist in Belgium for various purposes or districts, nearly all of which are federated in the Fédération Nationale des Sociétés d'Aviculture de Belgique, of which M. de Perre is the General Secretary. This great organization is recognized by the Government, and through it are chiefly directed efforts for the development of poultry-breeding. In addition to the grant for lectures (para. 100), already referred to, a subsidy of 7,500 francs (£300) is annually paid to the Federation, which is applied to the support of its work. The main points which are kept in view are (1) Instruction and Practical Experiments; (2) Improvement of Races of Poultry; (3) Compilation of Standards of Breeds; (4) Rules for and Lists of Approved Judges of Exhibitions; and (5) Dissemination of Information and Publication of Reports, &c. The Federation has also established a stud book, but there are many difficulties in the way of success. It is evident that what may be termed fancy poultry-breeding occupies a large share in the operations of the Federation, but certainly not to the exclusion of the practical side. It therefore exercises a wide influence, and is generally acknowledged to have done much for poultry-keeping in Belgium. The fact must ever be kept in view that it is a Federation of other Societies and not a Society with limited interests. Hence it must give effect to the wishes of those bodies whose representative it is. As fanciers' associations are more cohesive and active than utility societies the former naturally dominate. Grants are made of from 100 francs to 300 francs to various exhibitions; prizes are offered for the best poultry plants; enquiries and investigations are made as to various diseases and epidemics, and general assistance afforded in all sections. All poultry clubs or societies, whether for exhibition or utility poultry-breeding, are eligible for membership in the Federation, and have the right to elect one delegate for

every twenty-five members, the annual subscription being 5 francs for each delegate. There are now forty-six societies affiliated, with a total membership of 3,551, an increase of nearly 2,000 within two years. The Federation, which was instituted in 1898, to my personal knowledge has rendered very great service to Belgian poultry-breeders by organizing representative displays of the national races of poultry at the great international exhibitions of St. Petersburg, Madrid, Milan, and Rome, at which British poultry made so poor a show, with the result that a large amount of trade was lost to our breeders.

109. L'UNION AVICOLE DE LIÉGE.—One of the most enterprising of the local or district societies is that at Liége, which has as its President M. Braconnier, whom I had met previously at Madrid, and whose beautiful château at Modave, in the Ardennes, I had the pleasure of visiting. It is a large, powerful body with 900 members. At its headquarters is a fairly good library and museum. It has a veterinary surgeon who treats sick birds and makes investigations on behalf of its members. It receives no subsidy, but is liberally supported by subscriptions, and holds a large annual show. I am indebted to Mons. C. Wauters, the Secretary, for much information as to the work of this excellent society, which may be divided as follows : (1) Practical experiments upon a scientific basis, which are conducted under the supervision of the society, and the results compared and published. (2) Education, both by means of the library and lectures. (3) Publication of a weekly journal, which is sent post free to members who subscribe 5 francs per annum. This paper gives original articles and extracts from foreign publications. (4) Excursions of the members to visit practical and other poultry establishments in being. The annual exhibition is one of the most important in Belgium, and is well supported.

110. OTHER SOCIETIES. — Breed and district societies exist in considerable numbers as with us, the former of which are concerned chiefly in promoting the interest of the respective breeds. There are two Braekel clubs, one at Sottegem, under the presidency of M. Misirez, and the other at Renaix, whose President is M. Oscar Thomaes,

mentioned above. Whether this division of forces is due to local feeling, or other influences, it is not my business to enquire. At the other limit of the country is the " Société d'Aviculture La Herve," formed to promote the breed of that name. Many of these bodies are what is called " Unions Professionale," by which is meant that, subject to Government inspection of accounts, they receive a grant for installation of the office, but, except through the federation for special purposes, no annual subsidy. From what has been stated above it is evident that excellent organizations exist for promotion of the poultry industry of Belgium. Whilst on the one hand fanciers and utility poultry-breeders are in many cases working on antagonistic lines, and there is a serious danger in leaving the formation of standards of excellence to exhibitors, many of whom are extremists and do not care for the practical qualities, the advantages of bringing together in one federation all interested in poultry-breeding are very great indeed, though even under such circumstances utility men are less likely to be able to attend meetings than are fanciers. For that, however, the latter cannot be blamed. Belgium has done much for the poultry industry, and offers a great object-lesson as to what can be accomplished by intensive methods.

XI.—SUMMARY.

111. COMPARISONS.—Great though the differences may
be between Great Britain and Belgium, these are to a large
extent superficial, and are wholly overborne by the simi-
larities of conditions and needs.   That such is not the case
in America or Denmark was pointed out in my previous
reports, more especially as to the last-named country, where
production for export must be the main object of poultry-
keepers.   In many directions the conditions which demand
increased home production of eggs and poultry in the United
Kingdom are found to a greater degree in Belgium, where
this question has been faced, and, to a large extent, the
problem solved, whereas we are only in the early stages of
development, though much has been accomplished within the
last two decades.   *Pro rata* to its area the United Kingdom
is a densely populated country, but, as shown in Chapter I.
(para. 8), Belgium has 72½ per cent. more people to the square
mile than is the case with us, explained by the fact that her
rural districts have not suffered by depopulation as in Britain,
and that those who live on and by the land bear a much
higher relationship to the total of the entire country than is
now the case on this side of the North Sea.   During the last
generation the growth of industrial and commercial pursuits
has been enormous in both countries, the respective popula-
tions have increased greatly, wealth and purchasing power
have advanced with great rapidity, and, as a consequence,
the demand for all classes of food products is vastly greater
than ever before, whilst the rise in prices which has followed
such demand has not checked it in any way, due to the
corresponding ability to purchase, and the higher standards
of life of the working section of the community.   It will be
seen, therefore, that in these directions there are many points
of resemblance between the two countries.   Further, over
practically the whole of Belgium conditions are very similar
to those met with in the greater part of England, Wales, and
southern Scotland, where the producing districts are near to
the consuming population, affording facilities for sale which

are unavailable when eggs and poultry have to be sent over long distances. It must be recognized, however, that the Belgians have risen to their opportunities, so far as production is concerned, to an extent which is far in advance of Great Britain, which has enormously enhanced the prosperity of its rural districts. In this direction we find the greatest difference between the two countries. The Belgians have realized that intensification of production as a result of smaller occupations, which alone is capable of meeting the needs of a great consuming population without dependence upon extraneous supplies, whilst we are in the earlier stages of development on those lines. The result is that, practically speaking, Belgium is self-supporting in respect to eggs and poultry, for her small imports are more than covered by the exports to France and Germany, whereas Great Britain pays foreign countries £8,000,000 annually for these two articles of food. As an example of what can be accomplished on small farms, Belgium, with her numerous and prosperous people, affords every hope that the increase of small holdings in Britain will enormously advance the relative food production of the country in every direction. To accomplish that desirable end, similar methods must be adopted to those which are already met with in a few sections of England. I was informed that horticultural land is worth ten times as much in Belgium as ordinary farms, simply because production is tenfold greater.

112. CONCLUSIONS.—With a view to summarizing for the benefit of those concerned in the welfare of our rural community in general, and the extension of the poultry industry in particular, and ensuring the success of agricultural operations whether large or small, in which poultry-keeping is capable of contributing to an extent not hitherto realized, the following recommendations are submitted for consideration :—

(*a*) That a country which has a large industrial and commercial population, the majority of whom are unable to meet their own requirements in respect to eggs and poultry, can produce enough of both these articles of food without dependence upon foreign supplies, provided that the methods of poultry-keeping carried out are on lines calculated to secure the maximum of returns in accordance with the number of birds on each farm.

(*b*) That production is greater in relation to the acreage of the occupation where the farms are small in size, as there fowls can be kept at the lowest cost and receive that personal attention which is requisite to success. Consequently, special effort should be put forth to encourage poultry-keeping in those sections of the Kingdom where occupations are moderate in area, or small holdings are created, as in this way the prosperity of the individuals will be advanced and the national food supply increased. The instance cited, in Chapter III., of Sottegem, in which district the decline of handloom weaving was compensated by extension of poultry-breeding, offers an example how changes such as that named can be met by adoption of other pursuits.

(*c*) That with a view to the colonization of the uncultivated areas, of which there are nearly 24,000,000 acres in Great Britain, rather more than 42 per cent. of the whole country, the fullest encouragement should be given to the extension of poultry-keeping not only for immediate increase of supplies of eggs and poultry, but also as a rapid means of advancing the fertility of the soil and growth of ordinary crops. The evidence given in Chapter I. as to the remarkable changes which have taken place in the Campine near the city of Malines, where land practically useless is now being brought under cultivation as market gardens, due to the greater fertility of the soil as a result of keeping large numbers of poultry thereon, is of the greatest importance. There are many parts of our country capable of such improvement, which might be made productive and support a large and thriving population, were the opportunity afforded. This does not mean that larger farmers cannot keep poultry profitably, but that they are unable for various reasons to obtain equal results, except in the case of turkeys. Increased home production means lessened dependence upon foreign supplies, together with a hardier and more vigorous people.

(*d*) That, as in America and Denmark, and also Britain, the great bulk of eggs and poultry are produced on the ordinary farms and not at special plants, which, whilst they have a place in the poultry industry of any country, are more useful for the production of breeding-stock than of market supplies. Observations in Belgium have confirmed previous experience that the value of poultry farms is strictly limited in the direction indicated, and that the greater profit is secured by those who make poultry-keeping a part, albeit an important part, of their operations. At the same time it is possible to greatly increase production by specialization on lines such as at Lippeloo, described in Chapter IV.

(*e*) That in manufacturing and mining districts artisans can add substantially to their incomes by poultry-keeping, as in many parts of Great Britain, where land is available on reasonable terms, and every encouragement should be given to that class of producer who has the market for sale of eggs and poultry at his own door.

(*f*) That wherever public moneys are expended in promotion of the poultry industry, careful enquiry should first be made as to the class of poultry most suited to the district, and also the branch of poultry-keeping capable of yielding the greatest results. In Belgium this has been carried out more completely than in any other country I have visited. To some extent we have arrived at similar conclusions in Britain, though not to the same degree. The present report shows that almost everywhere egg production can be made profitable, but that the finest eggs are laid on the richer lands; that the same is true of fowl-breeding and rearing for table; that whilst table chickens can be reared on the poorer soils, a prime necessity for fattening is a plentiful supply of buttermilk, and, therefore, the dairying districts are where this branch should be encouraged; that duck-raising is specially suited to water meadows and fenlands, and that under such conditions natural food is abundant. Unfortunately communal land of that description is seldom met with; and that turkeys can be raised successfully in districts where slate or stone forms the bed. Given attention to these points, we may hope to see that uniformity of production within given districts which has only been apparent in a few sections of Great Britain. Were that the case more generally, the result could not fail to be satisfactory.

(*g*) That the production of milk chickens is essentially in Belgium, as in America, the business of those who keep the laying races of fowls, which grow much more rapidly than the heavier breeds, and are ready for killing at an early period. The doing so would provide a profitable outlet for cockerels, which are of small value when older, and would get rid of them ere they become troublesome. The breeding of these small chickens on a large scale has not proved profitable, and as the number from each producer must be small, it is desirable that all in the egg districts shall keep this branch of the trade in view so as to secure a regular supply during the period of demand.

(*h*) That there are manifest advantages in the keeping of a single breed of poultry over any area where the conditions are similar, so as to secure uniformity of produce. In many parts of Great Britain, and to a lesser extent in Ireland, the conditions are very varied, but where that is not the case the present mixture of races is undesirable. It would, of course, be essential that a selected breed should be one which had proved itself most suited to the district.

(*i*) That Belgians have proved that the most prolific layers of eggs are those which are small in size of body, and their best laying hens weigh 4 lb. or less. Therefore all efforts to enlarge our laying races of fowls for exhibition purposes should be resisted, as tending to reduce the productiveness. Further, that with intensification of method the cost of production will probably rise, and therefore the careful selection of breeding stock is imperative with a view to greater average production.

(*j*) That a modification of the system of importing chickens from Italy as egg producers, described in Chapter III., might be introduced with advantage. There is no reason why the breeding of such birds in some districts of the United Kingdom should not be carried out on an extensive scale by farmers, selling these to purchasers in other sections of the country.

(*k*) That whilst artificial methods of hatching and rearing are not adopted in the egg districts, where comparatively few birds are hatched on the individual farms, in the table poultry districts the period of hatching is greatly extended, and the introduction of these appliances has led to a great extension of the industry, which is also true in one of the duck districts. It is desirable that the system of rearing chickens in glass houses, which is recommended in the Londerzeel district, should be given a careful test.

(*l*) That efforts should be put forth to develop the production of large winter fowls similar to the *poulets de Bruxelles*, and the soft roasters of America, both on the part of the farmers and at special plants on the system adopted by Vicomte de Beugham at Lippeloo, which latter forms a central hatching and rearing station in combination with farmers who keep the breeding stock on one hand and fatteners on the other. These could be conducted on co-operative lines similar to the newly formed establishment at Street, Somerset.

(*m*) That there are many sections of the country where the production of small or squab turkeys for sale during the summer might be introduced. A profitable trade for these could be created without much difficulty.

(*n*) That in view of the decreasing foreign supplies of eggs, and, so far as can be seen, the improbability that there are any new sources for good-quality produce likely to be opened, it is of supreme importance that every effort should be put forth by central and local authorities and by individual farmers to advance poultry-keeping on progressive lines in the United Kingdom. In Belgium the winter average appears to be higher than with us, and it is essential that attention should be given to this question, as the shortage of supplies from October to December is very serious indeed. What has been done in Belgium can surely be accomplished here.

(*o*) That the offering of prizes (1) for poultry on farms, and (2) for the best individual displays at Christmas markets, is worthy of consideration as a means of stimulating the adoption of better methods, and of increased production. The first of these has been done on a limited scale by one or two county councils, but it is capable of great extension.

(*p*) That the markets in our great cities require to be re-organized in view of the great increase of population, with a view to securing freedom of trade for producer and buyer. Such is specially true in London, where Charters granted two or three hundred years ago prevent expansion in accordance with present-day needs. And that by local authorities or co-operative organization markets or auctions for the sale of poultry, or fairs, as at Ronquières, should be established in suitable districts. Further, that the time has arrived when producers must have greater control over sale in markets by having accredited agents for sale of their eggs, poultry, etc.

(*q*) That experiments should be undertaken on several points mentioned in this Report, notably as to the feeding value of rye-meal for egg production, of buttermilk for fattening, and the use of various weeds with the parasites thereon for ducks and poultry generally, as well as in many other directions.

(*r*) That in all our developments simplicity should ever be kept in view, as applied to breeding, rearing, and feeding, so as to secure the greatest result at the least possible cost.

EDWARD BROWN.

Regent House, Regent Street, W.,
February, 1910.

INDEX.

"A Stolen Harvest," 58
Abbeys, Influence of, 9
Abnormal Types, 8
Acknowledgments, 3
Advanced Methods, 6
Age of Hens, 33
Agricultural Colleges, 93
,, Country, An, 2
Allotments, Poultry, 32
Alost, 44
An Old Pursuit, 41
Antwerp, Province of, 5, 9, 11, 26
Archery Contests, 65
Ardennes Fowl, 83, 85
Area of Belgium, 11
Artizans and Poultry-keeping, 33
Auctions, Poultry, 79
Audenarde, 22, 26, 28, 55, 71, 73, 76, 79
Average Egg Production, 38
Axioms on Poultry-keeping, 33

Bantams for Utility, 87
Barter in Sale of Eggs, 74
Belgian Luxemburg, 5, 10
,, Races of Poultry, 80
,, State Railways, 98
Belgium a Huge Poultry Farm, 10
,, Poultry-breeding in, 5
Bevere, 56
Black Braekels, 61
Blue Termonde Duck, 83, 89
Brabant Fowl, 82, 85
,, Province of, 5, 11
Braconnier, M., 100
Braekel Clubs, 32, 100
,, Country, The, 27
,, Fowl, 38, 82, 84
Braekels, 29, 31
Breeding Farm, A, 32
,, Farms, 45
,, Theories, 90
Breeds, Distribution of, 82
,, for Milk Chickens, 42
,, of Ducks, 89
Bresse Fowls, 41
Brooders, 52
Brooder Houses, 23, 51
Bruges Game Fowl, 21, 85
Brussels Markets, 77
Buckwheat, 24
,, Meal, 49
Buff Orpington Fowls, 32
Burgenhout, 22, 44
Burgomaster of Ronquières, 66

Buttermilk for Fattening, 44, 49

Cages for Fattening, 48
Campine Fowl, 34, 38, 82, 84
,, The, 14, 22, 34, 55
Canary Breeding, 7
Carpiaux, M., 96
Census, Poultry, 13
Changed Conditions, Effect of, 37
,, District, A, 15
Charlemagne, Time of, 8
Chickens from Italy, 17, 36
,, on Water Meadows, 29
Children a Source of Riches, 27
Clean-shelled Eggs, 34, 73
Climate, Effect of, 80
Cock-crowing Contests, 88
,, fighting, 8
Coffee in Water, 24
Colony House System, 21
Colour of Eggs, 37
,, of Shells, 74
,, of Under-plumage, 91
Communal Land, 60
Comparisons, 102
Conclusions, 103
Consumption in Lancashire, 72
Co-operation, No, 72
Coops, 22
Cost of Fattening, 50
,, Food, 23
,, Production, 106
,, Rearing, 54
Courtrai, 26, 30
,, Fowl, 82
Cows and Poultry, 20
Cramming not Adopted, 48
Crowing and Fecundity, 89
Crushing Table Poultry, 43

Dairying and Poultry-keeping, 28
Dairy Schools and Poultry-teaching, 95
Dari, 24
de Becker, M., 66, 67, 68
de Beughem, Vicomte, 9, 50
de Mulder, M., 13, 73, 75
de Perre, M., 99
Decline of the Goose, 64
Demand for Produce, 102
,, for Turkeys, 65
Density of Population, 12
Dindon des Grains, 68
Diphtheritis, 19, 36, 47
Disease, 19, 34
Disease as a Result of Tainted Soil, 47

Disposal of Turkeys, 68
Distribution of Breeds, 82
Dockweed for Ducklings, 59
Drouillon Frères, 61
Duck-breeding, 55
Ducklings and Chickens, 56
   ,,   Feeding of, 60, 62
   ,,   Hatching and Rearing, 21
Ducks and Water, 91
   ,, with Poultry, 18

Ear-lobes, Colour, 84
Early Hatching, 46
East Flanders, 26, 28, 43
Egg-farming, 35
   ,, Hampers, 74
   ,, Markets, 73
   ,, Production, 23, 26
Eggs, Clean-shelled, 34
   ,, Imports and Exports of, 16
   ,, Packing the, 74
   ,, Size of, 29
Electric Light in Villages, 97
Enclosures for Ducklings, 61
Enfeeblement in Turkeys, 68
Escaut River, 28, 29
   ,, Valley of the, 55
Exhibitions, Belgian Peasants and, 33
   ,, in Belgium, 8
Experimental Work, 95
Exports, 3
   ,, of Eggs and Poultry, 16
   ,, to France and Germany, 41
External Characteristics, 83

Fair, A Turkey, 69
Families, Large, 27
Fancy Poultry, 7
Farm Poultry-keeping, 10
   ,, Work, 27
Farms at Renaix, 31
   ,, Poultry, 9
Fatteners, 45, 47
Fattening Ducklings, 62, 63
   ,, Establishments, 47
   ,, of Malines Fowls, 95
   ,, of Merchtem Ducks, 95
   ,, Turkeys, 69
Fédération Nationale des Sociétés
d'Aviculture de Belgique, 92, 95, 99
Feeding, 23, 53, 60, 62
   ,, Experiments, 95, 108
   ,, Table Poultry, 49
Feeding Young Turkeys, 68
Fertility of Land, Improved, 14
Few Turkeys, 64
Feyaerts, M., 51
Firm Yolks, 75
Flanders, 5, 11, 13, 22, 26, 55
Flavour of Ducks, 90
Flemings, 5
Flemish Proverbs, 11, 23
Fontenoy, 61
Forms of Poultry Houses, 19

Fowls and Improvement of Soil, 14
French Flanders, 5
Fruit Growing, 26

Game Fowl, 82
Geese, 83
   ,, Breeding, 64
Gembloux Agricultural College, 93
General Conditions, 5
   ,, Management, 18
   ,, Notes, 97
Germany, Trade with, 43
Ghent, 55
Glasshouses for Rearing, 46
Gouter Matrimonial, 69
Grammont, 28, 73
Grants for Lectures, 92
Grasheide, 15, 20
Great Eastern Railway Company, 98
   ,, Western Railway Company, 98
Gregoire, Professor, 96

Haeltert, Plant at, 10
Hainaut, 55
   ,, Province of, 5, 21
Halles Centrales, Brussels, 79
Hatching, 21, 46, 51, 57
   ,, Time of, 18
   ,, Turkeys, 68
Herve Fowl, 36, 83, 86
   ,, The, 22, 25, 35
Historical, 8
Holdings, Size of, 29
   ,, Number of, 12
Homing Pigeons, 7
Horses and Poultry, 20
Housing, Methods of, 18, 19
Hubert, Mons. C., 93
Hungarian Eggs, 75
Huttegem and District, 55
   ,, Duck, 83, 89
   ,, Fowl, 21, 57, 82

Illustrated Poultry Record, 30
Imported Eggs, 39
Imports, 103
   ,, of Eggs and Poultry, 16
Improvement of Races, 90
In-breeding, 84
Increased Number of Poultry, 11
   ,, Production, 6, 36
Incubators, 18, 21, 46, 61
Industrial Developments, 2, 6
Industry, The Duck, 55
Instruction in Poultry-keeping, 92
Intensive Production, 2, 6
Introduction, 1
Italian Fowls, 17
   ,, ,, as Layers, 36
Italy, Chickens from, 36

Keerbergen, 15
" Kickefritters," 8
Killing Fowls, 43
   ,, Table Poultry, 50

Kizmotin, M. Louis, 48
Koorman, M., 48

Lacroix, M. Leon, 94
Laloux, M. Maurice, 4
Lancashire, Consumption in, 72
Land, Improved Fertility of, 14
,, Rent of, 33
Languages Spoken, 5
Laplaigne, 26, 60
,, Duck, 83, 89
La Société les Célébataires Repentants, 70
Lebbeke, 44, 60, 62
Lectures on Poultry, 92
Leghorn Fowl, 36, 83
Leghorns, White, 9
Lentille de l'eau, 59
Liége, 39, 55
,, Province of, 5, 10, 37
Light Railways, 97
Lille, 5, 30, 39, 71
Limbourg, Province of, 5
Linen Weavers, 28
Lippeloo, 9, 22, 50
Little Compton, R. I., 11
Local Breeds, 80
Londerzeel, 11, 22, 44, 71
L'Union Avicole de Liége, 95, 100
Luxembourg, Belgian, 5, 10

Maize, 24
,, Effect of, 75
Making Animals Breed, 91
Making Hens Lay, 40
Malines, City of, 43, 44, 73
,, Fowl, 32, 42, 77, 82, 84
,, Market, 77
Manure Beds for Ducklings, 62
,, Use of, 14
Markets, 44
Market at Audenarde, 76
,, Gardens follow Poultry, 14
,, Poultry, 41
Marketing Restrictions, 107
,, the Produce, 71
Matrimony, Turkeys and, 69
Meat for Ducklings, 62
Merchtem, 22, 44, 60, 62
,, Duck, 83, 89
Methods Adopted, 45
,, at Laplaigne, 61
,, of Housing and General Management, 18
,, of Turkey-breeding, 67
Meuse, Valley of the, 55
Michotte, M., 66
Milk Chickens, 41, 105
,, Sheep, 24
Minister of Agriculture, 3, 93
Minorca Fowls, 32, 37, 82
Modern Developments, 6

Namur, Province of, 5, 10, 37
Nation of Poultry-breeders, A, 27
National Federation of Poultry Societies, 99
Natural Food, 23, 56
Nearness of Markets, 71
Nederbraekel, 28, 73
Netherlands, Prosperity of, 9
New Breeds, 81
,, Introduction of, 8
New Methods of Rearing, 107
No Co-operation, 72
North to South, Influence of, 82
Note of Warning, 47
Notes on Eggs, 75
Number of Holdings, 12

Objects of Enquiry, 1
Odour of Eggs, 76
Old Hens, Sale of, 46
Opwyck, 44
Orpington Fowl, 32, 42
Ottignies, 26
Overcrowding, 20

Packing the Eggs, 74
Parasites on Dockweed, 59
Pauwels, M. Robert, 87, 88
Pays d'Alost, 5, 11, 13, 27
Perches, 20
"Philosophers" at Ronquières, 65
Plaskie, M. Joseph, 44
Population of Belgium, 12
Portable Houses, 19
Poulets de Bruxelles, 1, 26, 43
,, *de Grains*, 42
,, *de Lait*, 41, 83
Poultry and Increased Fertility of Land, 104
Poultry-breeding in Belgium, 5
,, Farm at Lippeloo, 50
,, Farms, 9
,, for Market, 41
,, Imports and Exports of, 16
,, Keeping in Belgium, 1
,, Market at Audenarde, 76
,, Number of, 13
,, Schools, 94
Preservation of Eggs, 74
Prices, 107
,, of Eggs, 17, 24, 39
,, of Table Poultry, 54
,, of Turkeys, 69
Prizes at Archery Contests, 65
Production, Average Egg, 38
,, in Relation to Size of Farms, 104
,, Methods of, 1
,, Value of, 13
Profits, 51
Prosperity follows Poultry, 15
,, of Belgium, 3
Puers, 44
Putte, 15, 34

Qualities of Races, 83

Rabbits, 7, 34
" Races of Domestic Poultry," 6, 83
,, of Poultry, Belgian, 3, 80
Racquet, Professor, 93
Railway Rates, 98
Range of Tours, 2
Rates, Railway, 98
Rearing, 22, 46, 51, 57
Removal of Breeds, Effect of, 81
Renaix, 10, 22, 28, 30, 39, 71, 73
Rent of Land, 33
Results, 2
,, at Lippeloo, 54
Ronquières, 65
,, Turkey, 26, 90
Roubaix, 30
Roup, Prevention of, 18
Rumpless Fowls, 86
Runs for Growing Birds, 53
Rye, Effect of, 75
,, Meal, 24
Rymenam, 15

Sale of Turkeys, 66, 68
Sandy Soil and Poultry, 14
Schollaert, the Hon. F., 3
Shape of Eggs, 75
Shaping Table Poultry, 50
Sheds for Ducklings, 63
Silver Braekels, 31
Simple Methods, 18
Simplicity Essential, 108
Single Breed over Given Area, 106
Sitting Hen and Smell, 91
Sixteenth and Seventeenth Centuries, 9
Size of Body and Fecundity, 106
,, ,, Prolificacy, 83
,, Eggs, 36, 37
,, Fowls, 40, 43
,, Holdings, 12
,, Ronquières Turkey, 67
Skill in Breeding, 6
Slates on Perches, 20
Small Area, 71
,, Farms, 5
,, Poultry-keepers, 105
,, Turkeys, 68, 107
Smell of Sitting Hen, 91
Sottegem, 11, 22, 28, 39, 71, 78
South to North, Influence of, 82
Spartan System, A, 58
Special Poultry Plants, 105
,, ,, Schools, 94
Standards of Life, 6
State Agricultural Colleges, 93
Statistical, 13
Stock-breeding, 6]
Straw Coops, 22, 57
,, House, 20
Sugar-beet Growing, 66
Suitability of Breeds to Districts, 81, 105

Summary, 101
Supplied Foods, 24
Syndicates, 73

Table Poultry, 10
,, Area, 44
Tainted Soil, 47
Termonde, 43, 44
Thimister, 23, 25
Thomaes, M. Oscar, 32
Time of Hatching, 18, 33
Tournai, 30
Trade and Navigation Returns, 17
,, Guilds, 6
Trap Nesting, 33
Trappist Monastery, Poultry at, 9
Treading for Worms, 59
Tributes in Fowls, 8
,, Poultry, 66
Trough Feeding General, 49
Turkey-breeding, 64, 66, 67
,, Fair, A, 69
,, -headed Malines Fowl, 45, 85
Turkeys, 83
,, and Matrimony, 69
Typical Examples, 31

Uncultivated Land, 104
Utility Bantams, 87

Value of Production, 13
,, Table Poultry, 45
Van Gelder, M., 88
Van Schelle, Madame, 3, 10
Vanden Borchacht, M., 15
Vander Snickt, M. Louis, 3, 4, 30, 37, 43
Varied Conditions, Effect of, 80
Vicinal Railways, 97
Villa des Poulets, Renaix, 32
Virtou, 64
Vise, 64

Walloons, 5
Water Lentils, 59
,, Meadows, Braekels on, 29
,, ,, for Ducks, 56
,, for Ducklings, 58
Wauters, Mons. C.
Wavre, 38
Weertz, Mons. L., 94
Weights Increased by Fattening, 49
,, of Ducklings, 61
Western Brabant, 26
West Flanders, 26, 28
White Malines, 85
Wiers, 64
Winter Eggs, 39
,, Fowls, 43, 107
,, Supplies, 74
Worms for Ducklings, 59

Yolks of Eggs, 75

CPSIA information can be obtained
at www.ICGtesting.com
Printed in the USA
BVHW05s1227300718
523023BV00026B/1125/P

9 781330 733547